DIGITAL FINANCIAL INCLUSION

With the arrival of the 'Internet of Things' (IoT), smartphones, real-time payments systems, plus FinTech activity, Financial Inclusion services can now be integrated into a country's National Payment System (NPS), which means there should be no systemic barriers to transitioning the socio-economic pyramid, as actors build their financial status. This, however, is not the case. This book is a comprehensive guide to understanding the transition of financial services from cash-based to digital-based systems, with a focus on Financial Inclusion.

It explores the success of Financial Inclusion programs in promoting economic activity and lifting people out of poverty. It does not concentrate on a single deployment or approach, rather, it takes a broader view. The book surveys the technology and infrastructure required to build digital payment systems, as well as the regulatory and governance frameworks that enable their operation, however, the major focus is on the incorporation of these financial services within communities in order to deliver social outcomes. The book opens the conversation, proposing a new method of measuring Financial Inclusion. It takes a critical but constructive look at the field over the last 20+ years and discusses the key learnings. It examines the Kenya mobile money approach to Financial Inclusion, compared with the Indian bank lead approach, and delivers a broad-based plan on how the programs can be more effective in the future.

Financial Inclusion requires a pathway to progress, through a period of technology transformation. The foundation is provided by this book and the reader, on finishing it, will have a comprehensive appreciation of the subject matter.

Peter Goldfinch is the founder and Principal Consultant for Goldfinch Advisory in Victoria, Australia.

DIGITAL FINANCIAL INCLUSION

Towards Inclusive and Sustainable Finance for All

Peter Goldfinch

Routledge
Taylor & Francis Group

LONDON AND NEW YORK

First published 2025
by Routledge
4 Park Square, Milton Park, Abingdon, Oxon OX14 4RN

and by Routledge
605 Third Avenue, New York, NY 10158

Routledge is an imprint of the Taylor & Francis Group, an informa business

© 2025 Peter Goldfinch

The right of Peter Goldfinch to be identified as author of this work has been asserted in accordance with sections 77 and 78 of the Copyright, Designs and Patents Act 1988.

British Library Cataloguing-in-Publication Data
A catalogue record for this book is available from the British Library

Library of Congress Cataloging-in-Publication Data
Names: Goldfinch, Peter, author.
Title: Digital financial inclusion : towards inclusive and sustainable finance for all / Peter Goldfinch.
Description: Abingdon, Oxon ; New York, NY : Routledge, 2024. | Includes bibliographical references and index.
Identifiers: LCCN 2024001243 (print) | LCCN 2024001244 (ebook) | ISBN9781032748191 (paperback) | ISBN 9781032748207 (hardback) | ISBN9781003471073 (ebook)
Subjects: LCSH: Electronic funds transfers. | Finance—Technological innovations. | Finance—Technological innovations—Social aspects.
Classification: LCC HG1710 .G64 2024 (print) | LCC HG1710 (ebook) | DDC 332.1/78—dc23/eng/20240123
LC record available at https://lccn.loc.gov/2024001243
LC ebook record available at https://lccn.loc.gov/2024001244

ISBN: 978-1-032-74820-7 (hbk)
ISBN: 978-1-032-74819-1 (pbk)
ISBN: 978-1-003-47107-3 (ebk)

DOI: 10.4324/9781003471073

Typeset in Sabon
by codeMantra

CONTENTS

FIGURES

TABLES

ACKNOWLEDGEMENTS

The author's appreciation goes to Ross McIntyre from Payment Consulting Network for undertaking a review of this book and making useful recommendations.

The author also appreciates the encouragement and support Anthony Howard and Marie Tamplin gave him to write opinion pieces, originally named the *Goldfinch Report*. This led to the author writing his first book, *A Global Guide To Fintech And Future Payment Trends*, and subsequently this book.

The author also acknowledges the support of his family Kay, Jeff, Steve, and Ness who unwittingly came along for the ride. A ride that took them to various parts of the world from one of the most remote countries, New Zealand.

1

FOREWORD

It is important to ensure the readers' expectations with respect to this book are established correctly.

The Financial Inclusion premise assumes that effective and efficient financial services delivered through the digitalization of money will stimulate economic activity and bring people out of poverty. Those at the bottom of the socio-economic pyramid will be able to move out of poverty, through the increase in economic activity, supported by money transfers, savings, micro-credit (loans), micro insurance, etc.

The author's underlying proposition for achieving this objective of Financial Inclusion is through delivering financial services to all the layers of the socio-economic pyramid with an integrated National Payment System (NPS) within each jurisdiction. This does not mean all use cases will be common to all socio-economic pyramid layers. The actor facing <u>dialogue</u> and the processing pathway for payment instructions will vary depending on differing factors such as those based on environmental and infrastructural capabilities.

This book examines whether the Financial Inclusion programs delivered over the last two decades have been successful at a macro level. The book also examines varies options with respect to a road map for achieving a higher level of success. The book is not a study of how effective individual programs have been in targeting specific challenges of individual communities. There have been programs deployed targeting specific community challenges with a non-inclusive approach. These are often referred to as closed loop solutions. Solutions that do not support interoperability across all communities in a jurisdiction. Inadvertently, these programs entrap their targeted community by prohibiting mobility up the socio-economic pyramid through restricting commercial activity.

DOI: 10.4324/9781003471073-1

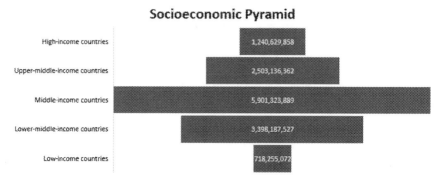

Socioeconomic Pyramid

High-income countries	1,240,629,858
Upper-middle-income countries	2,503,136,362
Middle-income countries	5,901,323,889
Lower-middle-income countries	3,398,187,527
Low-income countries	718,255,072

FIGURE 1.1 Socio-economic Pyramid

When developing a community-based payment solution it should be undertaken in compliance with industry standards to facilitate the capability to integrate with the jurisdiction's NPS. The NPS may not yet be formally established at the time of deployment, but the assumption must be made that in the lifetime of a payment solution it will be established.

This book examines Kenya and India's individual approaches to developing a financially inclusive NPS. Kenya NPS essentially developed organically, whereas India's approach has been more structured and planned in line with global practices.

This book refers to the socio-economic pyramid based on income categories. What does the pyramid really look like? Using World Bank population data, the pyramid is not quite a pyramid as represented in the above graph. Significant percentage of the world population resides in the middle income layer. This books focus is on the lower-middle and low-income categories or approximately 30% of the world's population (Figure 1.1).

Permissions

ITU Facts and Figures: Focus on Least Developed Countries and World Bank Global Findex Database 2021, are used to support the relevant propositions, etc. It is the understanding that these organizations have undertaken best efforts to ensure the data is an accurate as possible but there are obviously no guarantees.

ITU request that those using their data make the following statement:

"This translation was not created by the International Telecommunication Union (ITU). ITU is not responsible for the content or accuracy of this translation. The original English edition shall be the binding and authentic edition".

2

CURRENT ASSESSMENT

The Financial Inclusion focus is on banking the world's 1.4+ billion world citizens who remain classified as unbanked. The prerequisite for an individual to becoming financially included is having a transaction account for the storage of digital/electronic money. This does not necessarily mean that all those with an account are financially included. The transaction account must be actively used on a regular basis for the account holder to be truly included. A more realistic indicator is to measure the volume of electronic funds transferred between the accounts of two unique actors. In simple terms, the growth in payment transaction volume will directly lead to reducing poverty. Activity levels are a more accurate measurement of inclusion.

A transaction account will not reduce poverty itself but having an account is the first step in enabling participation in an economy.

The CGAP Strategic Directions FY 2019–2023 view reinforces this position: '*Empowering Poor People to Capture Opportunities and Build Resilience through Financial Services*'. Effectively saying once a person is banked, then they can take themselves out of poverty assuming capability to identify, create, and exploit an opportunity.

The core requirement across all sectors of an economy is firstly being paid (receiving money), then avoiding excessive charges that erode the amount received, and finally the speed of the process. Critical considerations are trust and security. Having a transaction account addresses these issues to varying degrees but not completely. Many in some justifications will claim bank charges are too high, the process takes too long, especially in comparison to cash. The payment industry refers to the friction having to be low.

An ineffective and inefficient payment (money transfer) system impacts businesses of all categories, government agencies, as well as other actors

DOI: 10.4324/9781003471073-2

regardless of financial status; however, the lower socio-economic transaction account holders are far less financially resilient to sustain slow and costly money transfer services.

The following table looks at the growth of accounts firstly by income category and by region, between 2011 and 2021 (Table 2.1).

The table below demonstrates significant increases in the number of accounts across all categories. Those with a low level in 2011 show the highest percentage of growth with the Sub-Saharan Africa achieving an outcome of 139%. This situation illustrates a stage 1 success in a two-stage process. The second stage is activity.

Table 2.1 also shows the level of inactive accounts for 2014 and 2021. Overall, the world percentage has dropped from 9% to 5%. The negative is that the level of activity across the lower income categories remains high with the low income increasing 3-fold from 11% to 34%. This is a three fold increase. South Asia remains high at 32% for 2021.

It can also be asked whether the percentage that use their account only once when opened and not again. If this is a significant percentage then why?

Therefore, the challenge is still to discover the reasons for accounts being inactive so a strategy can be developed to shift them to being truly active.

TABLE 2.1 Accounts by Income and Region

Income Categories	Accounts		% Growth	% Inactive Accounts	
	2011	2021		2014	2021
High income	88%	96%	9%	2%	2%
Low income	10%	39%	345%	11%	34%
Lower middle income	30%	62%	107%	23%	24%
Middle income	43%	72%	67%	12%	13%
Upper middle income	57%	84%	47%	6%	3%
Regional Categories					
East Asia & Pacific	72%	83%	15%	6%	3%
Europe & Central Asia	69%	90%	30%	3%	1%
Latin America & Caribbean	39%	74%	90%	5%	6%
Middle East & North Africa	38%	53%	39%	N/A	7%
North America	89%	95%	7%	0%	0%
Sub-Saharan Africa	23%	55%	139%	7%	5%
Arab World	22%	40%	82%	14%	10%
Euro area	90%	99%	10%	2%	1%
South Asia	32%	66%	106%	31%	32%
World	51%	76%	50%	9%	5%

Source: World Bank Group, World Bank Group – Global Findex Database

Nature of Transaction Account Usage

Usage can obviously be measured on a sliding scale between accounts being only a receptacle for receiving funds (i.e., remittances, wages etc.) to being fully transactional accounts used for daily purchases utilizing a digital payment delivery channel. Funds held in an account for a short term until converted to cash is not truly the use case for being financially included. Using a transaction account for the accumulation of a balance (savings) is arguably a use case for being financially included, although it implies cash is still being used for everyday payments.

Savings do not necessarily drive economic growth although economists undoubtedly will argue with merit that savings held by a financial institution facilitates lending and investment. Investment leads to economic growth. The savings history of a borrower improves their credit rating through demonstrating a capability to meet repayment obligations.

The following Table 2.2 provides a high-level view of usage regarding mobile accounts sourced from the World Bank Global Findex Database 2021 covering adults (15+ years). This chart illustrates that although mobile money accounts are spread across all the income categories except 'high income', usage is higher for the low-income category which indicates the impact being made by mobile payment services for those that have a mobile money account. The issue is those with an account is only 27% (Table 2.2).

Cash payments do stimulate economic growth; however digital payments increase the velocity of the money flow and therefore deliver a greater stimulus than cash. There is a strong argument that cash is far more costly to an economy although generally actors do not recognize the cost. Obviously, it is efficient in a person-to-person situation.

It is extremely difficult to measure the impact of Financial Inclusion in the short term on economic growth, as there are many influencing factors. It could be argued the impact on well-being should be measured, which is a more nebulous concept. The World Health Organization in referring to mental health define well-being as a state "…..*in which every individual realizes his or her own potential, can cope with the normal stresses of life, can work productively and fruitfully, and is able to make a contribution to her or his community*". This is without doubt what the Financial Inclusion programs are attempting to achieve.

Financial Inclusion Country Index (Alternative Indicator)

As mentioned, the current quantitative method of measuring Financial Inclusion is through the number of citizens with a bank account. As stated, it is more important to measure the flow of funds through the accounts, the digital transaction levels. A high cash conversion rate, whether through an

TABLE 2.2 Mobile Money Transaction Spread

	High Income	Low Income	Upper Middle Income	Middle Income	Lower Middle Income	World
Account	96%	39%	84%	72%	62%	76%
Mobile money account	0%	27%	10%	12%	14%	10%
Use a mobile money account two or more times a month (% with a mobile money account)	0%	17%	4%	7%	9%	6%
Store money using a mobile money account (% with a mobile money account)	0%	14%	3%	5%	7%	4%
Saved money using a mobile money account	0%	13%	2%	3%	4%	3%
Borrowed any money using a mobile money account	0%	5%	1%	2%	2%	1%
Made a utility payment: using a mobile phone (% who paid utility bills)	28%	40%	15%	16%	17%	19%
Received wages: through a mobile phone (% of wage recipients)	0%	24%	7%	9%	12%	7%
Received government transfer: through a mobile phone (% of government transfer recipients)	0%	0%	17%	13%	9%	9%
Received payments for agricultural products: through a mobile phone (% payment recipients)	0%	17%	0%	7%	8%	–

Source: World Bank Group, World Bank Group – Global Findex Database

agency or ATM network, reflects a poorly developed and/or untrusted digital payment acceptance network.

Taking the lead from the GSMA, measuring funds through a transaction account provides a clearer picture of the transitioning from cash to digital and digital to digital. *The GSMA State of the Industry Report on Mobile Money, 2022* stated that cash-in to mobile money systems amounted to USD261 billion while cash-out was USD178 billion. In simple terms, 32% remained in the system to cover digital payments and savings.

In exploring an alternative method of determining a country's level of Financial Inclusion, an indexing table was built using the data in the *World Bank Group - Global Findex Database, 2021*. The method of scoring is based on taking the level of accounts and building an index based on the level of usage of those accounts. This does mean that a country with a low level of citizens with accounts could have a high score if the usage level is high.

The result should only be treated as indicative, but the scores do pass the creditability test. The top 10 countries fit a demographic profile with nine having an adult population of less than 10 million. GDP per capita levels are respectable except for Mongolia standing out as particularly low at USD4.2 thousand and Norway the highest at USD77.8 thousand. Small in terms of population and geographical size maybe a determinant (Table 2.3).

The following is the index by the World Bank country income categories. The interesting factor is there is a sizable gap between lower middle income and upper middle income. There is undoubtedly a barrier between these two income levels which is likely to be based on the ability to adapt (or access) to technology (Table 2.4).

TABLE 2.3 Financial Inclusion Country Index

	Index	Adult Pop (mls.)	GDP per Capita (USD,000)
Top 10 countries			
Estonia	7.4	1.1	23.8
Latvia	6.6	1.6	17.6
Denmark	6.6	4.9	61.0
Norway	6.6	4.5	77.8
Czech Republic	6.5	9.0	23.1
Sweden	6.4	8.5	51.4
Singapore	6.3	5.0	65.4
Slovak Republic	6.3	4.6	19.3
Mongolia	6.3	2.3	4.2
Iceland	6.2	0.3	66.8
Finland	6.1	4.7	49.6
Bottom 10 countries			
South Sudan	0.07	6.6	n/a
Afghanistan	0.11	22.6	n/a
Niger	0.25	10.4	n/a
Lebanon	0.27	5.1	8.80
Sierra Leone	0.32	4.8	n/a
Iraq	0.32	25.0	5.60
Pakistan	0.34	144.0	1.40
Egypt, Arab Rep.	0.37	67.6	3.00
Nicaragua	0.47	4.7	1.90
West Bank and Gaza	0.55	3.0	n/a

Source: World Bank Group, World Bank Group – Global Findex Database

TABLE 2.4 Income Classification

Low income	1.06
Lower middle income	1.57
Middle income	2.93
Upper middle income	4.97
High income	5.85

Source: World Bank Group, World Bank Group – Global Findex Database

Comparison of the Two Extremes

Figure 2.1 provides a visual view of the top 5 countries in comparison to the bottom five and places Finance Inclusion in perspective. A key point is that the top five countries have a high uptake of financial accounts and associated debit cards. This is not unexpected (Figure 2.1).

Velocity Measurement

The Velocity of Money formula is defined by Madhuri Thakur @ Velocity of Money Formula|Calculator (Examples with Excel Template) (educba.com)

> The velocity of money can be defined as the speed at which money flows in an economy. In simple terms, we can describe the velocity of money as the speed at which money is being spent in an economy to buy goods and services. It can either be a dollar, a euro or any other currency spent to purchase these goods and services. Income earned by an individual enables them to purchase more freely which tends to increase the money velocity.

The velocity of money tells us how people hold cash or spend it. If there is a fear of losing a job, the person will spend slowly. On the other hand, if a person feels she/he has enough money, then she/he will tend to spend it faster. The economy that shows faster movement in money can be considered as a healthy economy. This may stimulate inflation and central banks will increase interest rates to reduce spending. However, the economy expands if the payment transactions increase and consequently shrinks when fewer payment transactions are made. Velocity of money is never constant. As stated, central banks increase interest rates to decrease inflation.

How is the Velocity of Money calculated?

The change in money velocity is mainly due to two reasons:

- Change in the economy's GDP
- Change in the money supply

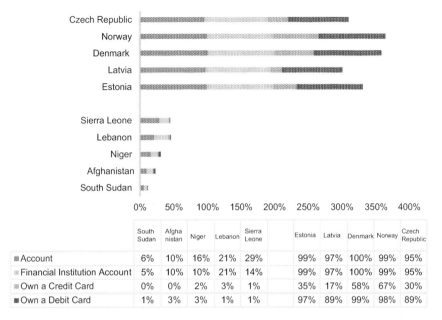

	South Sudan	Afgha nistan	Niger	Lebanon	Sierra Leone		Estonia	Latvia	Denmark	Norway	Czech Republic
Account	6%	10%	16%	21%	29%		99%	97%	100%	99%	95%
Financial Institution Account	5%	10%	10%	21%	14%		99%	97%	100%	99%	95%
Own a Credit Card	0%	0%	2%	3%	1%		35%	17%	58%	67%	30%
Own a Debit Card	1%	3%	3%	1%	1%		97%	89%	99%	98%	89%

FIGURE 2.1   Account Ownership - Two Extremes

Source: World Bank Group, World Bank Group – Global Findex Database

Thus, the velocity of money is simply calculated by dividing the money supply with the economy's GDP.

Certain factors that influence the velocity of money are the value of
money, volume of trade, frequency of the number of transactions, and the
credit facilities, among others.

A payment system (network) should be viewed as an enabler of commerce. A well-developed digital payment system will improve business activity across all communities. An approach to measuring the impact that digital
payments are having on an economy is to measure the velocity of money
within a community. This is possibly the only means of determining if a fully
banked population with an effective and efficient digital payment system is
stimulating their economy and therefore lifting people out of poverty.

Financial Inclusion – Holistic View

The early advocates for Financial Inclusion seem to have been disconnected
by not taking a holistic view. Their theories and hypotheses did not seem
to consider the realities that the targeted unbanked sectors are members
of a broader jurisdiction, and for financial inclusion programs to make an
impact on the jurisdiction's well-being a significant percentage of the jurisdiction's actors must change their behaviour. Money will flow into individual

communities within a jurisdiction, circulate within, and a percentage will flow out. You might argue that if the amount of money that is circulating within a jurisdiction is increasing, the financial health or prosperity of the jurisdiction is also improving. The financially excluded will migrate into the included sector though needing to be a community participant and having a transaction account is the determinant or enabler.

As with the barter system, cash as a payment method can also be considered to have a limited capability regarding improving a jurisdiction's wellbeing. This is because it fails to drive the circulation of funds at a pace that will stimulate economic growth down to the lower levels of the socio-economic pyramid, necessary to improve total wellbeing. This same argument is also applicable (to a lesser extent) for any payment system that has a 24 hour (or next day) clearing circle. Accounts are often debited in near real-time with the credit only being posted to the recipient's account the next business day. Addressing this issue is one of the benefits of an NRT system. The **Near Real Time (NRT) Payment** method is covered in this book. Ignoring any barter system, the payment systems of a jurisdiction must transcend the following phases. Usually, at a different pace for each unique community.

Level 1: Funds are received in cash and are held until used for a cash payment(s). Surplus funds are often deposited with an informal financial institution or simply retained and stored as cash.

Level 2: Funds are received in cash and stored in a digital form within a transaction account provided by a formal financial institution. For payment, funds are converted back into cash. Surplus funds may stay in the account or can be alternatively withdrawn and deposited with an informal institution.

Level 3: Funds are received in a digital form into a transaction account provided by a financial institution. To make a payment, funds are accessed and transferred in a digital form. Surplus funds remain in the transaction account or are moved into a savings account but stay within the formal system.

Financial institutions can be prudential or non-prudential formal. The expectation is that the formal institutions will dominate in the higher levels of the socio-economic pyramid. Mobile money services registered with a jurisdiction's regulatory would be considered as formal but not necessarily a full service.

When communities move through and adopt the next level, rarely do the previous level's behavioural practices cease completely. Usage of the previous level practices obviously diminish as the community becomes more digitalized. In any economy, certain payments may be for various reasons considered cash-suitable. The more financial inclusive a community becomes, the greater use of payment methods classified as belonging in level 3, above. Transition will be gradual.

The Kenya experience is being examined from a transitional perspective. Refer to Kenya Provides a Template 7.1

Learning from the Past

Those working in the financial inclusion sector are obviously committed, but many have worked in a self-imposed bubble. The past is not being used as a guide to the future. All highly financial inclusive ecosystems (jurisdictions/communities) started from a low level of Financial Inclusion. It could be claimed their economic base was stronger than the emerging economies of today and it was just a case of adopting the technology as it became available. This is probably a rather simplistic view as not all technologies were adopted quickly, if at all. Often solutions were introduced without a clear user proposition and being based on immature technology were unable to deliver on their promises.

It can be argued the countries that embraced financial inclusion early were held back waiting for suitable technology to be delivered to enable deployment. Technology in many cases digitalized manual or mechanical processes; however, they were not always successfully. It could be claimed that because the successful technologies were introduced over time, they were accepted more easily. In contrast, today communities have a smorgasbord of services, being continuously updated. This may be delivering a negative impact rather than being a progressive driving force for socio-economic development. Continuous or rapid change does not necessarily deliver the best outcome for payment services, as new payment methods require jurisdiction acceptance. Acceptance at a high enough level to deliver a return on the investment will only be achieved over an extended period. Investors often are required to take a long-term view, accepting that changing actor behaviour, regardless of the strength of the proposition is not immediate.

ATMs proved an almost instant success; however, point of sale (POS) acceptance took up to two decades before in many jurisdictions it achieved significant transaction volume. ATMs dispensed cash: POS eliminated cash. Even today, in the most digitized economies a significant percentage of the population will still be committed to using cash.

The following Table 2.2 again is derived from the World Bank Global Index Database 2021, presenting a digital cash dependency index covering the corresponding bottom and top jurisdiction.

The bottom ten countries are those that have the lowest dependency on cash (Table 2.5).

The chart below shows the position of the World Bank income categories. The level of the low-income category is a reflection of the state of their economies. Predictably the low-income category is the most dependent on cash and as income increases the dependency on cash drops significantly (Figure 2.2).

The slow adoption of Financial Inclusion can be blamed on a range of reasons such as cost, trust, KYC, access to agents, and financial literacy but

TABLE 2.5 Cash Dependency Index

	Cash Dependency Index		
	Cash Index	Adult Pop (ml.)	GDP Per Capita (USD)
Top 10 Countries			
Bosnia and Herzegovina	0.96	1.1	23.8
Serbia	0.96	2.3	4.2
Bulgaria	0.86	1.6	17.6
Moldova	0.78	4.5	77.8
Thailand	0.78	4.9	61
Ukraine	0.77	8.5	51.4
Philippines	0.75	42.3	31.8
Romania	0.75	9	23.1
Indonesia	0.72	4.7	19.3
Sri Lanka	0.71	4.9	49.6
Bottom 10 countries			
Netherlands	0.02	4.8	N/A
Canada	0.02	11.5	1.6
South Sudan	0.02	3	N/A
Iceland	0.02	4.7	1.9
Denmark	0.01	25	5.6
Finland	0.01	67.6	3
Austria	0.01	144	1.4
Belgium	0.01	5.12	8.8
New Zealand	0.01	6.6	N/A
Norway	0.00	22.6	N/A

Source: World Bank Group, World Bank Group – Global Findex Database

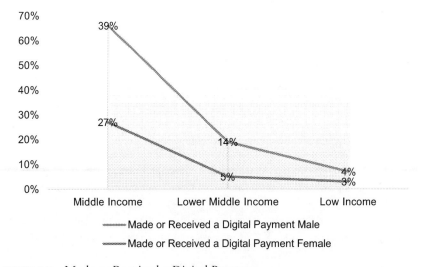

FIGURE 2.2 Made or Received a Digital Payment

Source: World Bank Group, World Bank Group – Global Findex Database

rarely are mentioned reasons such as the avoidance of tax, hiding wealth especially from government authorities, hiding income earned from illegal activity, etc.

Learnings from the top ten payment jurisdictions should not be disregarded. In addition, the learnings from newer entrants such as Kenya, India, Bangladesh, etc. are also critical. These learnings allow the development of a strategy for Financial Inclusion to enable advocates to develop a road map for the transitioning of actors up the socio-economic pyramid.

Current Global View

The World Bank's Global Findex Database (2021) as demonstrated provides the Financial Inclusion advocates with a wealth of data. It allows us to compare the level of Financial Inclusion participation by income levels (as well as comparing regional geographies plus country-to-country comparisons).

The following is a table of key indicators across income categories:

Table 2.6 clearly shows those on a lower income are more likely to have a mobile money account than the other categories, but the percentage is still low (27%). The lower income group has also a higher-than-expected account with a financial institution (24%). This indicates one of two factors or a combination of both. Mobile money accounts are not universally available plus they are not fully meeting the needs of their account holders. Further the low-income and lower-middle-income groups received a significant level of 'sent or received' remittances.

There is apart from these individual indicators an expected contrast between the income levels when it comes to initiating a digital payment. The index shows the high-income category participation rate in the digital

TABLE 2.6 Key Indicators by Income Category

	Mobile Money Accounts	*Financial Institution Account*	*Debit Card Ownership*	*Made or Received Digital Payments*	*Has an Inactive Account (% with an Account)*
Lower income	27%	24%	10%	35%	3%
Lower middle income	14%	58%	27%	38%	15%
Middle income	12%	70%	46%	57%	9%
Upper middle income	10%	84%	68%	80%	2%
High income		96%	86%	95%	1%
World	10%	74%	53%	64%	7%

Source: World Bank Group, World Bank Group – Global Findex Database

economy far exceeds the middle and lower-income categories. This is likely to be a case of affordability and the ability of individuals to adapt to new technology. Without doubt due to a higher education level covering both financial management and technology.

Observations

More low-income actors have a higher percentage of Financial Institution accounts than Mobile Money accounts (24% vs 18%), and in specific countries such as Kenya significant percentage of actors do have both types of transaction accounts. Just 4% of middle-income actors have a mobile money account whereas the high-income actors are not registering as having a mobile money account. Expectantly, 96% of this category do have a financial institution account.

For low income, 21% of transaction account holders are reported to have initiated a digital payment and 28% have been a recipient of a digital payment. High-income transaction account holders' percentages are 87% and 67% respectively.

When an actor increases their financial inclusiveness, are they required to cross the divide between the mobile money providers and the financial institutions? By staying with only a mobile money service, are they trapped in the economic sector serviced primary by mobile money providers, therefore inhibiting their abilities to transition up the socio-economic pyramid? Does this create a two-speed economy?

This book does not specifically answer this question but the reader on completing the book should have a view about where crossover services are essential to achieving a high level of Financial Inclusion leading to the migration of actors up the socio-economic pyramid and out of poverty. Technocrats will argue correctly that this can only occur by developing interoperability between the services. There is also the issue of the bank branch networks not reaching out to those actors traditionally residing at the lower socio-economic levels. This has led to the development of agency networks. The Indian financial inclusion program is heavily dependent on banking correspondent organizations, who have developed an agency network(s), and this is proving to be successful.

At a strategic level, the situation drives the need for a broad base national payment system (NPS) that integrates the various financial services as if one.

Statistics and Considerations

Generally, the statistics for this book have been sourced from both the World Bank Group – Global Findex Database and the ITU, Measuring Digital Development Facts and Figures. Focus on Least Developed Countries March 2023 report. Having up-to-date data is critical in measuring the impact of the

Financial Inclusion programs. Lower-level statistics can also be sourced from in country and often government providers. However, there is a time lag.

Two countries (India and Kenya, although not exclusively) have been selected to illustrate the various alternative approaches and trends. The rational for their selection is the level of Financial Inclusion activity (past and present) targeting a sizable unbanked population. Further, the author considers their contrasting approaches are critical for the readers to understand the available options. Each jurisdiction needs to develop a Financial Inclusion strategy that best fits their circumstances.

Kenya has a high penetration of mobile accounts, which is indisputable. However, the Philippines has a particular low level of mobile accounts reported in the World Bank Global Findex Database, although Smart Money (now PayMaya) and GCash have been in the market sense 2001 and 2004 respectively. The Philippines mobile accounts may be categorized as financial institution accounts as the MNOs have relationships with the card schemes and their domestic issuers.

Ideally, we need to understand by category the number of payments made per person over a 12-month period. A single transaction over a calendar year does not really mean an account is active. Using an indicator such as the suggested 'index' provides a macro measurement at a jurisdiction level. It enables a league table to be established which has some value.

Geography Determines Financial Inclusion Status

Financial Inclusions is an objective for many jurisdictions, but only ten based on the World Bank Global Findex Database (2021) are claiming a 100% banked population and another 9 claiming 99%. There are another 21 countries above 90% and 17 below 40%.

An important point is not only do these 17 jurisdictions below 40% need to set Financial Inclusion objectives, there are several developed jurisdictions who need to consider how to minimize their respective unbanked populations.

As pointed out previously, the level of transactions per account is critical. There is no point in an actor having a transaction account with an inactive status or having irregular usage.

National Payment & Transportation Systems Face Similar Challenges

To support producers there is both the need for an efficient distribution network (supply chain) and payment system. Receipt of a payment(s) through the distribution chain allows producers to fund their businesses. This is most important for SMEs and sole traders including primary producers who do not necessarily have access to working capital that is available to larger businesses. Accessing loans to cover short-term funding requirements is often not an option, regardless of whether the business is operating in a developed or emerging economy.

The apparent commonality between transport and payments became apparent to the author when introduced to a business in the southwest of London whose prime source of income originated from modelling truck deliver routes for a supermarket chain, enabling them to maximize the efficiency of their networks. This modelling business prior to the author's visit had closed out a contract to use their technology and knowledge to model payment messages for a central bank to achieve the same outcome.

Poor or non-existent transportation links restrict economic development. Producers need to deliver their products to market in a timely manner to achieve in the case of agriculture the best prices. Developed transportation links enlarge the marketplace for producers. This enables producers to increase their output, achieve greater economies of scale, and reduce their costs to enable them to be more competitive. Obviously, underdeveloped transportation networks restrict the producer's ability to sell to a larger market and therefore the ability to grow their business.

The point being made is a country's payment infrastructure is as critical to its economic as other infrastructure components such as transportation. There is no point improving levels of productivity unless the shipping of goods to market is efficient and the payment system is trustworthy to ensure producers/manufacturers are being paid in a timely manner.

Transport networks require a set of rules and controls to be in place to ensure traffic flows and accidents are kept to a minimum. The payment system of any country demands the same disciplines. This is where standards and regulation come into effect.

The payment system is therefore a critical component of a national economy. Commence is severely inhibited if an efficient supporting payment system has not been deployed.

Dr. Jean-Paul Rodrigue and Dr. Theo Notteboom in their publication: 'Transportation and Economic Development | The Geography of Transport Systems' (transportgeography.org) make a valid point that access to resources and being able to operate more efficiently improves competitiveness. Receiving payments within a commercially accept timeframe is a key input for enabling to operate efficiently.

The thesis put forward is the payment system is as critical as the transportation network to commerce. Both networks can be physical or virtual (digital). There should be no argument that a financial system underpins economic development. Payments are a core element of the financial system in terms of the exchange of value.

Efficient payment systems are a key infrastructure for economic development.

Reference to: Carlos Martínez Sarnago and Àlex Ruiz March 11th, 2014 in their publication: www.caixabankresearch.com/en/economics-markets/

financial-markets/payment-systems-key-infrastructure-economic-develop-ment, a similar point is made that payments which are comprehensive, efficient, and secure ensure that money transfer improves the consumer confidents.

It is a basic assumption and general agreed opinion that improvements in the payment system leads to greater economic development.

An instruction to make an electronic payment generates a sequence of messages that flow down communication links to switches that reroute the messages either to another switch or to the destination, which in most cases is a transaction account held by a financial institution. The response will be returned most likely but not necessarily down the same route to the originator of the instruction. Funds will be transferred between transaction accounts.

Payment networks have the same problem with congestion that occurs on transport links. At certain times volume will increase well above the norm. Both networks must be developed to handle the peaks. So therefore, the planning processes for both is very similar.

Theoretical Understanding

Payment is the activity or process that supports (or enables) commerce. It is not the 'main act' but if payment cannot be made the commercial process will fail.

The following diagram illustrates the generic steps related to making a purchase and the positioning of payment in the process (Figure 2.3).

Obviously, the duration of each step relates to the type of product and service being purchased, and in the case of supermarket shopping you might make several purchases but only one payment. You might argue there is no negotiation, but you might select a brand/product based on the price as well as quality.

The biggest change in commerce has come from the emergence of the Internet and e-commerce. E-commerce could be argued as the Internet enabling mail order and catalogue sales channels to broaden their target market through digitalization. The payment providers, especially the card schemes were late in recognizing the front-end payment process needed to be re-engineered, so PayPal and similar services moved into the space. This should be a lesson to the established providers, adapt quickly, or miss opportunities.

NPS Integration

There have been several Financial Inclusion projects in emerging markets, funded by NGOs and development organizations targeting a specific need without taking a wider view. Some short-term gain is often made, but mass-market adoption fails to eventuate. The primary reasons are these new payment services are not being built to support the needs of a targeted market in a manner that supports integration into a broader payment network.

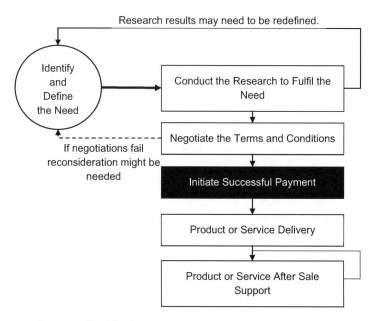

FIGURE 2.3   Payment Positioning

The Indian Reserve Bank has shown a considerable amount of leadership to drive the development of an affordable payment system into their country's rural regions. Vietnam is another country also developing in a coherent manner. The Central Banks of Iran and Iraq both have the view that a national network compliant to international standards must be deployed. The Iran payment system is ranked high on the Index in comparison to many countries over previously surveys but has dropped positions due to sanctions.

However, the norm has been to see disparate payment systems being implemented where there is little consideration for interoperability, especially integration at the domestic level but equally importantly internationally. Reverting, back to the transport analogy, would you build a road that does not connect to the national network of roads? So why would you build a payment service that does not connect to the NPS.

Many may point the finger at East Africa; the author would point the finger at the mobile payment sector in general although we have seen positions mature. The GSMA in there, State of the Industry Report on Mobile Money 2022 recognize the importance of mobile money integration with the broader payment system.

After recording exceptional growth in 2020, the value of transactions flowing between banks and mobile money platforms also grew quickly in 2021, up 46 per cent, more than doubling since 2019. The continued acceleration of these types of transactions confirms the complementary relationship between banks and the mobile money industry that has been observed in the past few years, confirming mobile money's key position in the financial ecosystem.

Future Projections

Futurists must develop a well-reasoned view of the future direction of payment systems to satisfy the demands of changing commercial business models. For payments with so much noise being made by the FinTech advocates, it is important for the sector to develop a rational future view, a road map to enable new developments to be placed in context. Development in context with the objectives of a growing economy. With the aim of supporting the elimination of the lower levels of the socio-economic pyramid.

Futurists must not be afraid to be proven wrong, although in most cases it is the timing that is likely to be wrong, not the outcomes. Futurists are likely to be overly optimistic in this industry. The previous Governor of the RBA, Philip Lowe in his Address to the Australian Payments Network Summit, 9 December 2021, made the following projection of the future of payments by highlight five trends that are evident in the payments system. Being:

1 Increase use of electronic forms of payment
2 Higher usage of digital wallets
3 Involvement of 'big techs' in payments
4 Development of new business models impacting payments
5 Community greater interest in security, reliability, and cost of payments

With payment transactions migrating away from batch processing to near real-time processing, the business model for financial institutions (inclusive of banks) is shifting away from the traditional silo model where specific accounts and delivery channels were developed for a specific service. This occurred organically rather than as a define strategy because there was no clear road map of where technology would take commerce and therefore where commerce would take banking and therefore payments. With a greater level of enlightenment, the banks working with business clients are in a position to develop and deploy more modular systems that can be easily integrated to deliver new or enhance services.

Consequences for Financial Inclusion

By understanding the digitalization of payment systems in the developed economies, Financial Inclusion programs will stay current by following. Financial Inclusion must be a follower not a leader as this carries the risk of being isolated especial if the developed economies unexpectedly evolve in another direction.

A concern especially for Financial Inclusion is technology advancements are not only disrupting the current payment systems but also delivering uncertainty regarding the future view.

Mobile money systems developed in the first decade of this century, now into their third decade are considered legacy systems. They could be referred to as the first generation. Financial Inclusion progress will be slow if there is a need to re-engineer previous generations of systems because they are supporting outdated technology which make them unsustainable.

Impact of Financial Inclusion on Economic Growth

One of the propositions of Financial Inclusion is the positive impact in terms of stimulating economic growth. If this is the case, to what degree is not necessarily easy to measure. Logic suggests as more actors enter the workforce the greater the need to be financially included. Logic also suggests as more actors participating in an economy the faster the GDP will growth.

Kenya's increase in both per Capita GDP and percentage of those with accounts between 2011 and 2021 was based on a growth rate between 45% and 49%. Not too much should be read into this but there must be a correlation.

The following table is based on data extracted World Bank Global Index Database 2021 and illustrates the growth from 2011 to 2021 by each of the income categories (Table 2.7).

Table 2.7 illustrates an interesting trend. A significant percentage of the middle-income categories have an account with a non-financial institution. Derived from the percentage with an account compared to those that have an account at a financial institution. Will this trend continue? Is it because younger members of a family have adopted mobile money requiring the older adults to have an account as well to facilitate the transfer of funds?

TABLE 2.7 Account Holders by Income Category

Income Levels	Account			Financial Institution				
	2011	2021	Change	2011	2021	Change	2011	2021
High income	88%	96%	8.3%	88%	96%	8.3%	–	0%
Low income	10%	39%	74.4%	10%	24%	58.3%	–	27%
Lower middle	30%	62%	51.2%	30%	58%	48.2%	–	14%
Upper middle	57%	84%	32.1%	57%	84%	32.1%	–	10%
Middle income	43%	72%	40.2%	43%	70%	38.6%	–	12%

Source: World Bank Group, World Bank Group – Global Findex Database

The maturing of the population over ten years in terms of employment/income must also be considered as a factor.

It maybe because mobile money service providers have recently started to expand their suite of financial services for customers, including saving and loan products via mobile money accounts. The analysis based on transaction level data from Kenya confirms that mobile money customers are indeed starting to use new financial services, with about half of the mobile money accounts in the study being used for such transactions. These findings also point to the importance of accurate measurement of mobile money activity, especially for the central bank policymaking, as mobile money continues to expand into other streams like credit.

Bibliography

Central Bank of Kenya in Collaboration with Kenya National Bureau of Statistics & Financial Deepening Trust, 2019/20/21 FinAccess Household Surveys.

CGAP, The CGAP Strategies Directors FY 2019–2023, 31 May 2018.

GSMA, State of the Industry Report on Mobile Money, 2018/2019/2020/2021.

Hasan, De Renzis and Schmiedel, Retail Payments and the Real Economy, *European Central Bank*, 12 August 2013.

IBEF Blog, India ADDA – Perspective on India, Promoting Financial Inclusion Through Policies, September 22, 2021.

ITU, Measuring Digital Development Facts and Figures: Focus on Least Developed Countries, March 2023.

Rodrigue, Jean-Paul and Theo Notteboom, Transportation and Economic Development, in *The Geography of Transport Systems*, edited by Jean-Paul Rodrigue, New York: Routledge.

Sarnago, Carlos Martínez and Àlex Ruiz, Payment-Systems-Key-Infrastructure-Economic-Development. caixabankresearch.com

Thakur, Madhuri, @ Velocity of Money Formula|Calculator (Examples with Excel Template).

World Bank Group, World Bank Group - Global Findex Database, 2014/2021.

3

SOCIAL OBJECTIVES SUPPORTING FINANCIAL INCLUSION

This chapter examines the rationale behind the Financial Inclusion thinking and asks if the objectives are being realized. Statistics published by the World Bank will be used to support the various views.

There are two opposing approaches to viewing Financial Inclusion, which are not necessarily in conflict as one has a demand side view and the other a supply side view.

Ethan Loufield, in a blog post on the Centre for Financial Inclusion website, titled, 'The Business Case for Financial Inclusion: A Multi-Trillion-Dollar Proposition', Feb 7, 2018, clearly states the purpose of Financial Inclusion.

> When we develop commercially viable financial services that can help low-cost private schools improve their facilities, smallholder farmers increase crop yields, families afford solar energy, and entrepreneurs improve sanitation (just to give a few examples), we are effectively steering money into the basic life needs that really are prerequisites for authentic, long-term business growth. Our ability to cultivate new markets that can sustainably grow well into the trillions of dollars is ultimately predicated on our ability to improve the human condition. At the end of the day, this is why the future of Financial Inclusion is about much more than financial services.

The same website published an older article in June 2013 by Sonja Kelly, and Elisabeth Rhyme, titled, 'Growing Income, Growing Inclusion: How Rising

DOI: 10.4324/9781003471073-3

Incomes at the Base of the Pyramid Will Shape Financial Markets'. To quote from this report:

> Real incomes are rising among the currently poor, moving hundreds of millions of people from more extreme levels of poverty into levels at which they begin to have some income flexibility. This change will provide the opportunity for a fast-growing uptake in financial services if providers can effectively meet the needs of this emerging vulnerable class. These changes are taking place at different rates in different regions and countries, with important implications for Financial Inclusion.

These two quotes raise the question of which comes first, economic growth or Financial Inclusion. In the first case, Financial Inclusion contributes to economic growth and the second view is that economic growth is necessary to transition people out of poverty. Economic growth is necessary to achieve Financial Inclusion.

A key point is that the members of 'vulnerable classes' need financial services to transition out of poverty but also without Financial Inclusion they cannot maintain and improve their well-being.

The urban/rural perspective is a critical factor with Financial Inclusion. It is a reasonable assumption to claim that in the urban environments there will be financial services available, established for those in the high-income brackets. The point in terms of Financial Inclusion is how these established services can be connected to those who are considered as belonging to the vulnerable class, the lower levels of the socio-economic pyramid.

Those that are in the vulnerable class, even in an urban environment, are most likely to live in a district that is poorly serviced. Those in the lower socio-economic levels are also unlikely to engage with financial institutions who deliver services to the higher income, higher socio-economic levels. Entering a branch can be a stressful experience for those less knowledgeable regarding financial services and are less familiar with the social etiquette associated with banking.

The author when undertaking a study relating to banking correspondents in India spoke to one provider who claimed their success was based on opening agencies in the poorer urban districts where the agent was part of the community. The agent was open during the times the workers were at home rather than during standard business hours. The agent was one of them and so was trusted. This is a simple example of servicing a financial sector not accustomed to using formal financial services, specifically a branch network.

Understanding the simple nuances of the customer base is a requirement to achieving commercial success.

For the rural environments, formal financial services may not exist, as the services may not have the geographical coverage. Informal financial services may be preferred or be the only available service. To deliver retail banking to the lower socio-economic levels, the service providers must be attuned to the prospective account holder's social norms and expectations. The Indian banking correspondent model is an example of such an approach.

Digital Payments

If an actor lives in a cash dominated community, then physical cash is required. The actor has little option but to withdraw e-money as cash held in a money/transaction account to meet their payment commitments. A small balance may be held in their account as savings.

An argument based on facts cannot refute a near digital economy as it is more efficient (cost and time) and more effective if digital payment methods are embraced. The real challenge is how communities can transition from a cash economy to a digital economy. There is no clear road map to follow except that the proposition for digital transitioning must be strongly reinforced through incentives to encourage behavioural change. For example, fees for non-digital transactions such as charging cash handling fees should be considered. The future may see merchants surcharging to accept cash payments. This can only be justified once the digital payment network(s) reaches a broad coverage where most payments, if not all can be initiated through a digital channel.

However, there is a need to start, so why not by delivering transaction accounts for all and then evolve by driving the usage. This in effect has been the strategy to date, except the evolved usage part of the strategy, measured by the low level of active accounts is not yet proving effective.

The alternative is to create the need first for an account to be opened, and then it will be used. Remittances are a good example as are government payments. Government digital payments should be free of any charge and be immediate, whereas government cash payments as well as being delayed should carry a fee to recover the cost. Companies should also be given an incentive to pay their staff digitally through direct credits. In developed economies, the first signs of surcharging for accepting cash in retail stores indicates the realization that cash handling is costly. Retailers in some incidences are refusing to even accept cash payments.

Transaction account debits must go beyond cash withdrawals utilizing an agency or ATM network. Consideration must be given to paying merchants a small commission for accepting a digital payment. Australia did this with EFTPOS when it was first introduced by offering what was referred to as negative interchange. Internet and mobile digital bill payments are delivering significantly higher acceptance levels in developed economies. The convenience factor being the incentive for account holders.

A price needs to be placed on cash to change behaviour but not until the digital payment channels are operationally robust and broad based.

Informal Services

The path to full Financial Inclusion for many may be through the informal financial sector. The informal providers generally deliver a restrictive service covering both saving and credit facilities to small farmers, lower income families, and small businesses.

These services being community based are normally well trusted. They understand their customers, allowing them to service actors with poor or no literacy. Accounts can be opened without the need for formal identification. Obtaining credit is a simple process where approvals can be almost immediate.

The author while undertaking research in Nepal spoke with a senior banker who was discontinuing the bank's rural money transfer service. The bank was offering a free service based on the premise that account holders would retain savings in their bank accounts. This premise was flawed as account holders withdrew all their funds when their account was credited, then deposited the balance of those funds (after paying bills and purchasing supplies) with a local informal institution.

Using an informal institution cannot be assumed as a cheaper option. These institutions may charge depositors rather than pay interest. In effect, a negative interest rate as the funds will be held securely and in the case of women held safely as the money is unable to be accessed by their partners.

The informal sector is also known to charge high interest rates on cash advances. The lending is predominantly short-term, to minimize the lender's risk.

The champions of Financial Inclusion often claim that the criteria for success is that fees and charges must be low and therefore affordable to the financially excluded enabling them to adopt financial services. The factors that are possibly more critical to the providers of informal financial services are aligned with:

- A community connection that supports trust
- Availability of the service, based on customer's convenience
- The minimum of formality required to open an account or access a credit facility, supporting a customer base with low levels of literacy

The Indian bank-led solution offers a model that enables informal financial service providers to become participants in a national financial (inclusive of payments) system. This is critical to support the digital transfer of funds between categories of institutions.

In Kenya (and many other countries), there are SACCOs (Savings & Credit Co-Operative Society), who are licensed to meet the needs of the lower income population.

In general terms, SACCOs are savings and credit cooperative-owned and operated by and for its members, according to democratic principles. Their primary purpose is to encourage savings creating a pool of funds which can then be used to deliver loans to the membership. Interest rates are set at an affordable level. The objective is to deliver services that will improve their communities' economic and social well-being.

There is a firm belief that microfinance-lending enables poor families to overcome their liquidity challenges, providing the capability to invest in their farms, increase their productivity, and therefore transition out of poverty. Most SACCOs require the account holder to accumulate savings that in part can be held as collateral for a loan, those at the very bottom of the pyramid are not the market segment being targeted.

SACCO and microfinancing lenders cannot be assumed to be low cost. Interest rates may be low but there can be other charges relating to service fees, insurance cover, and the need to hold securities such as savings which all add to the borrowing cost.

There is evidence from Kenya that SACCOs are losing market share as alternative sources of borrowing are being introduced. Competition from the formal providers as markets are becoming more banked. However, SACCO market share, as reported from Kenya, does fluctuate possibly due to the economic conditions.

SACCO institutions are less likely to support the digital transfer of funds. Not supporting digital transfers will over time reduce their account holder proposition and therefore market share.

Bank Accounts and Activity Levels

The Financial Inclusion programs invariably when launched emphasize the opening of financial accounts for the financially excluded. This is considered the logical foundation block in building Financial Inclusion, but being an account holder does not strictly mean an actor is banked. It is one thing to have a bank account, it is another to use it. Being banked must be linked to usage.

MasterCard's Insights 'Digital Economy Last Mile' written by Dan Salazar, 22nd January 2019, informs us that 'person to merchant' payments globally are 37% digital, and the percentage in Sub-Saharan Africa and South Asia is apparently even lower in the range of 14–16%. Theoretically it could be claimed that if the population of a region/country is 50% banked then digital payments should be at a similar level, if not higher as early adopters should be more accepting of using digital payment channels.

There are distinctly different types of financial accounts being offered by the different categories of institution.

Financial institution accounts are more commonly referred to as traditional bank accounts. Reference is also made to mobile bank accounts. Maybe not in all countries but financial institutions in many countries are developing, if they have not already delivered mobile banking services that provide access all their account types. Financial institutions may also be offering a specific mobile account with specific attributes to meet the needs of customers. This is due to the adoption of the Internet as a service delivery channel supported by applications for a range of devices covering PC, tablets, smartphones, and even personal banking machines (PBMs) or ATMS. The line between internet banking and mobile banking in terms of the user experience is becoming blurred, as the underlying technology is similar across all the device types.

Non-financial institution accounts are offered by organizations that do not have a full banking license and consequently offer a restrictive banking service. Typically, these institutions have been established to deliver a service to a specific market segment. SACCOs and mobile money being two examples. Mobile operators offering mobile wallets to their subscribers are often subjected to restrictions applied by regulators such as the maximum allowable account balance and the maximum transaction value. These restrictions are not enforced on the financial institutions to the same degree. Financial institutions are normally subjected to a broader range of regulations, therefore are subjected to central bank oversight as they represent a systemic risk to a country's financial system in case of failure.

Conceptual View

It is far easier to conceptualize a Financial Inclusion model than to deliver a service with a high level of active accounts generating significant transaction volume, a service that delivers on the doctrine. There are obviously the technology issues just as those relating to the mobile network transitioning to 4G & 5G. This is been discussed in Chapter 5: 'Impact of Technology Advance on Existing and Future Services'. What is more difficult is the changing actor behaviour to enable a critical mass of active users to be established. This relates to the challenge of reaching the tipping point where mass acceptance takes over and drives volume. Identifying the market influencers can be important to changing actor behaviour. This may mean targeting the 20–35-year-olds, who have already been exposed to technology.

The author's view is a strategy must be established on developing all the elements of a Financial Inclusion ecosystem in unison, at a community level. Growth will be led by a few community champions who are early adopters.

Then a broader base of actors will organically evolve based on the community responding to a strongly endorsed proposition for behavioural change.

What is being asked of the financially excluded communities in emerging economies is to change their behaviour in a short period. The older actors from the developed countries have had decades to change their behaviour as the technology advances were introduced over an extended period (3 to 4 decades). The younger actors are born into an advance financially inclusive environment, having never experienced banking services that were not underpinned by technology.

An alternative strategy is making it increasingly difficult to use cash. This can be achieved by restricting its acceptance. This strategic approach most likely for political reasons would need to be undertaken slowly or by stealth.

The chart below illustrates the percentage of the population with accounts for each of the three years 2011, 2014, 2017, and 2021, by income category.

Growth in Bank Accounts

The signs are positive for the low classification in terms of citizens having a bank account. The lower middle classification has seen a drop in growth. However, account growth rates are meaningless if the new accounts have low activity levels and the funds are not retained in the account, as savings (if only for a short term) (Table 3.1).

The following chart covers the level of inactive accounts for the World Bank income categories. These percentages do not necessarily align with the claims made from many commentators, but it does depend on whether it is financial institution accounts or mobile money accounts or a combination of both. Often this definition is not clear or even mentioned (Table 3.2).

The chart above shows the percentage growth in accounts and the level of inactive accounts across the income categories for both 2014 and 2021 and

TABLE 3.1 Growth in Bank Accounts

	2011	2014	Growth	2017	Growth	2021	Growth
High income	88%	93%	5%	94%	1%	96%	2%
Low income	13%	23%	71%	35%	52%	39%	11%
Lower middle income	29%	42%	45%	58%	38%	62%	7%
Middle income	43%	58%	32%	65%	14%	72%	11%
Upper middle income	57%	72%	26%	73%	2%	84%	15%
World	51%	62%	22%	69%	11%	76%	10%

Source: World Bank Group, World Bank Group – Global Findex Database

TABLE 3.2 Inactive Accounts

	2014	2021	Change
High income	2%	1%	1%
Low income	11%	7%	–4%
Lower middle income	23%	24%	1%
Upper middle income	6%	3%	3%
Middle income	12%	13%	1%
World	9%	10%	1%

Source: World Bank Group, World Bank Group – Global Findex Database

the percentage change. The low-income category is the only one that is show-ing a significant positive shift. For the lower middle and middle categories, the inactive trend in accounts has marginally declined.

The number of accounts has improved across all categories, which is positive.

Source of Borrowing

The high-income group is a major borrower with the low and middle effec-tively being at a similar level. The low and middle-income groups are more likely to look to family and friends as a source of funds where the high-income group will access funds from financial institutions (including credit cards) (Table 3.3).

The lower income group is also more likely to sell an asset rather than bor-row, assuming that is an option. This is not necessarily positive, especially if the assets being sold are income generating.

The high-income actors are more likely to save (76% in 2021) and the pre-dominant reason is for old age (53%) with more than 58% using a financial institution. This contrasts with almost 44% of the lower-income category saving with 22% using the services of a saving club or a person outside the family. Only 42% of middle-income category are savers. The rationale for this may relate to a higher level of job security and the need to maintain a social position driving spending behaviour.

Deposited Funds

Logic tells us that if an actor has no source of funds (income) their account will be inactive, as the actor has no ability to spend. What are the sources that dominate?

The surprise credit transaction type is 'Deposit Funds'. Across income cat-egories those with a financial account are highly likely to make deposits. This

TABLE 3.3 Inactive Accounts

			Source of Borrowing			
	High Income	Low Income	Lower Middle Income	Middle Income	Upper Middle Income	World
Borrowed any money in the past year						
	65%	58%	46%	50%	55%	53%
From						
Financial institution	56%	9%	12%	22%	35%	28%
Credit card	51%			14%	27%	24%
Family or friends	14%	43%	33%	30%	28%	27%
Savings club		11%	4%	3%	1%	
Sale of assets	2%	14%	5%	4%	2%	4%

Source: World Bank Group, World Bank Group – Global Findex Database

TABLE 3.4 Deposited Funds

	With FI Account	Percentage Deposited Funds more than 2 Times
High income	96%	51%
Low income	41%	–%
Lower middle income	39%	10%
Middle income	57%	19%
Upper middle income	71%	30%
World	65%	25%

Source: World Bank Group, World Bank Group – Global Findex Database

implies that the account holders or another party on their behalf is depositing funds. The countries where account holders are least likely to deposit funds fall into the low-income category. The account holders from the other categories are potentially depositing their surplus cash into their accounts to build up their savings or is it just a secure repository? Alternatively, they may be receiving cash payments but have preference to initiate digital payments as a payer (Table 3.4).

Source of Income

The following chart is also based on the Global Findex Database, 2021, illustrating an alternative view to the socio-economic pyramid. The dependency on where income is sourced may determine social status in developing

TABLE 3.5 Source of Income

	Source of Income					
	High Income	Low Income	Lower Middle Income	Middle Income	Upper Middle Income	World
Domestic Remittances	0%	31%	20%	25%	30%	0%
Wages	55%	19%	23%	32%	42%	36%
Government Transfer	30%	6%	15%	15%	17%	19%
Public Sector Pension	20%	2%	6%	6%	8%	9%
Agriculture	0%	29%	14%	14%	6%	6%
Self Employed	0%	0%	0%	0%		

Source: World Bank Group, World Bank Group – Global Findex Database

economies. The high-income actor category has a high dependency on wages while the low-income actor category is significantly reliant on agriculture, domestic remittances and to a lesser extent on wages. The lower income categories in contrast to the higher income categories receive little in the way of government transfers.

This possibly reflects poor infrastructural and social development in rural economies covering other key government responsibilities such as transportation, education, telecommunications, health care, financial services, etc. (Table 3.5).

The following chart illustrates the level of cash payments received. Based on the World Bank Global Findex Database 2021, private sector wages dominate as the main source of cash payments. This is followed by agricultural income for all income categories except the high income category, where no percentage is recorded. It must be assumed in the more developed countries agricultural will largely operate on an industrial scale except for boutique producers and payments will be non-cash (Table 3.6).

It must also be assumed there is dependency of agricultural development on a digital payment system to ensure that producers are paid into bank accounts speedily and securely. The less developed countries where agriculture labour is hired on a more casual basis payment will be primarily cash. The chart above illustrated that agriculture and private wages are dominated by cash.

Remittances are reported by the Global Findex Database, 2021, as the highest source of income with the exception being again the exclusion of the high-income category (Table 3.7).

There are the two sources of funds, which must be paid into accounts for Financial Inclusion Programs to be successful. Government departments must ensure they can digitally pay salaries and benefits. Having an

TABLE 3.6 Source of Cash Payments

	Private Wages	Government Payments	Public Sector Wages	Government Transfers	Government Bension	Domestic Remittances	Agricultural Payments
High income	3%	1%	0%	1%	1%	0%	0%
Low income	4%	2%	0%	2%	2%	3%	0%
Lower middle income	8%	3%	1%	3%	3%	5%	6%
Middle income	11%	4%	1%	3%	4%	6%	10%
Upper middle income	8%	3%	1%	0%	0%	9%	20%
World	7%	3%	0%	2%	3%	0%	0%

Source: World Bank Group, World Bank Group – Global Findex Database

TABLE 3.7 Source of Domestic Remittances

	Received a Domestic Remittance	Money Transfer	Into an Account	Person to Person - Cash
Low income	31%	4%	18%	9%
Lower middle income	20%	2%	10%	6%
Middle income	25%	2%	16%	5%
Upper middle income	30%	2%	24%	3%

Source: World Bank Group, World Bank Group – Global Findex Database

account can be made a condition to receive a government payment for those actors in the catchment area of a Financial Inclusion program. That sounds simpler than it is, especially if the country does not have an NPS or it has one that is not connected to all financial institutions irrespective of type.

Firstly, government departments (authorities), who are responsible for originating payments must have the ability to generate direct credits to both financial and mobile accounts.

The table below shows this is happening, although the low-income categories' cash is still in the 20-percentage range. It should also be highlighted that the lower income actors are less likely to receive a government payment

TABLE 3.8 Method of Receiving Payments

	Received a Payment	*Received Through a Mobile Phone*	*Received into an Account*	*Received in Cash Only*
High Income	52%	0%	84%	3%
Low income	11%	27%	52%	26%
Lower middle income	21%	8%	56%	21%
Middle income	25%	16%	78%	9%
Upper middle income	23%	12%	67%	15%

Source: World Bank Group, World Bank Group – Global Findex Database

TABLE 3.9 Agricultural Payments

	Received a Payment	*To a Card*	*Received into an Account*	*Received Through a Mobile Pahone*	*Received in Cash Only*
Low income	29%	1%	23%	17%	69%
Lower middle income	14%	0%	19%	8%	71%
Middle income	10%	1%	35%	7%	60%

Source: World Bank Group, World Bank Group – Global Findex Database

as opposed to the higher income categories. This could have more to do with the country of residency (Table 3.8).

Requiring government payments into an account (account credit) must improve the actor proposition for the opening of an account. As demonstrated with respect to remittances in Kenya.

Agricultural Payments

Agriculture and self-employment are strong indicators of how far Financial Inclusion programs have penetrated an economy. It is key for agriculture because Financial Inclusion programs will facilitate farmers selling their products into an expanded market, improving their cash flow to grow more produce.

The table above (Table 3.9) shows the low-Income category and lower middle category in terms of agriculture have an extremely high reliance on cash for payment. However, the other categories (except High Income, not report) are not showing a positive position (Table 3.9).

Concluding Comment

The various data sources are only providing a very high-level representation, as they generally ask only if a transaction has been received and initiated in the past year, not how many times. Depositing of funds might only occur once or twice a year but wages could be daily or weekly, etc. generating higher volume of account credits over a 12-month period. Payment systems survive on volume, not generally on value except services established for high value transactions (processed by a RTGS), where fees often are calculated and charged based on the value.

The various statistics paint a picture that lower-income account holders do have a willingness, as demonstrated by deposited funds to maintain, and grow a balance in their accounts but potentially revert to cash for payments. This raises the challenge in providing access to funds when required at the convenience of the account holder in terms of timing and location. This access may be in the form of across the counter as cash (agent, or branch) or through a digital channel.

The statistics are also showing that financial inclusion programs are being used for P2P transfers of funds (direct credits) or domestic remittances. P2P may also be P2B, for particularly small businesses such as merchants.

Not All Negative

The following chart illustrates the digital payment impact by category income in terms of receiving and sending (initiating) digital payments (Table 3.10).

While the cash payments are still well entrenched across the income categories there is a reasonable and increasing uptake of digital payments. Knowing the number of transactions per account, per year (or preferably 30 days) is the required measurement of digital activity levels, and it will show the trends more clearly. However digital payment progression can be

TABLE 3.10 Receiving Digital Payments by Income Category

	High Income	*Upper Middle Income*	*Middle Income*	*Lower Middle Income*	*Lower Income*
Digital Payment Made	82%	76%	51%	30%	33%
Digital Payment Received	70%	52%	37%	52%	22%

Source: World Bank Group, World Bank Group – Global Findex Database

TABLE 3.11 Digital Progression 2014–2021

	High Income	Upper Middle Income	Middle Income	Lower Middle Income	Lower Income	World
Digital Progression 2014	88%	48%	36%	31%	12%	44%
Digital Progression 2021	95%	80%	57%	38%	35%	64%

Source: World Bank Group, World Bank Group – Global Findex Database

measured by comparing uptake across a reasonable range of years (Table 3.11). The following two graphs examine the uptake by income category and compares the bottom countries to the counties at the high end of the index table (Table 3.12).

Reason for No Financial Institution Account

The chart below clearly illustrates insufficient funds is the primary reason for not having a financial institution account. Cost and lack of documentation are secondary reasons. Across all the stated reasons, India singularly in comparison to the other countries addressed the challenges with a consistently low percentage for all reasons.

The message is that if the cost can be reduced along with the issue of insufficient or no documentation being resolved then the challenges of improving the level of Financial Inclusion can be minimized. Is this really the case?

The reasons progressively decline as the income level increases. This suggests that education and promotion by high profile respected individuals may be necessary to reassure lower income actors that the risks are minimal and lower than cash. Using sporting or entertainment stars to promote digital payments is not an uncommon practice.

At the beginning of this chapter, informal financial institutions were discussed. For a significant portion of the population, informal financial services are preferred over the formal services even if the costs are higher. This suggests that if there are other compelling reasons, they will override the concern of cost. In addition, a percentage of the population continues to maintain an informal account even when they have opened a formal account. As it has been suggested previously, account holders may be transitioning but is there a more underlying social reason to maintain accounts in both categories of financial institutions (Table 3.13).

TABLE 3.12 Digital Progression Gap

	South Sudan	Afghanistan	Niger	Lebanon	Sierra Leone	Estonia	Latvia	Denmark	Norway	Czech Republic	Sweden
Digital Progression 2014	88%	48%	36%	31%	12%	96%	78%	100%	99%	80%	99%
Digital Progression 2021	95%	80%	57%	38%	35%	99%	95%	100%	99%	94%	99%

Source: World Bank Group, World Bank Group – Global Findex Database

TABLE 3.13 Reason for No Account

	Upper Middle Income	Middle Income	Lower Middle Income	Lower Income
Insufficient Funds	12%	21%	29%	65%
Lack of Documentation	5%	9%	13%	32%
Lack of Trust	5%	8%	9%	22%
Religious Reasons	2%	3%	5%	8%
Someone in the Family Does	7%	10%	13%	10%

Source Data: World Bank Group – Global Findex Database

Mobile Accounts

The following chart for the lower-income account holders illustrates the comparison in the penetration level between financial institutions and mobile providers. In this chart, the contrast between high- and low-income categories is clear. With M-Pesa being the dominating service in Kenya, the overall market penetration level (those who have an account) is 70+% for the lower income population. The financial institution accounts penetration level is at 55+%. In India, in comparison, the financial institution accounts is at 80% for the same sector and mobile is almost not registering. This situation will be covered in the chapter titled 'Kenya and India, Opposing Approaches'.

A significant factor is that in all income categories except low income, financial institution accounts outnumber the mobile accounts. In the low-income category, it is 27% mobile and 24% financial institution. Does this indicate the other categories support the Indian-bank led approach of building a solid base and expanding this base as the pathway to success? The alternative view is that the Kenyan (M-Pesa) payments service was established to resolve issues associated with money transfer. It was originally and is possibly till date for most users a safe, low cost, and efficient service. Its success as a money transfer service cannot be disputed but is it a Financial Inclusion platform? The answer is probably no when a significant percentage of actors have both types of accounts (Table 3.14).

TABLE 3.14 Mobile – Financial Institution Gap

	High Income	Upper Middle Income	Middle Income	Lower Middle Income	Lower Income	World
Mobile	0%	10%	12%	14%	27%	10%
Financial Institution	96%	84%	70%	58%	24%	74%

Source: World Bank Group, World Bank Group – Global Findex Database

Table 3.14 shows the comparison of the two account types by income categories of Mobile Accounts to Financial Institution Accounts.

Bibliography

International Journal of Community and Cooperative Studies, Vol. 3, No. 2, pp. 1–56, June 2015.

Kelly, Sonja and Elisabeth Rhyme, Growing Income, Growing Inclusion: How Rising Incomes at the Base of the Pyramid Will Shape Financial Markets, June 2013.

Loufield, Ethan, Blog – The Business Case for Financial Inclusion: A Multi-Trillion-Dollar Proposition, clearly states the purpose of Financial Inclusion, 7th February 2018.

Salazar, Dan, Insights Digital Economy Last Mile, 22nd January 2019.

World Bank Group, Global Findex Database, 2021.

4
FINANCIAL INCLUSION FOR WOMEN

There has been a focus on growing financial inclusion for women. CGAP's following statement places Financial Inclusion for women in focus.

"We also aim to explore women's formal and informal income-generating opportunities that add value to women's lives and livelihoods leveraging digital solutions."

Women's Financial Inclusion: A Pathway to Women's Economic Empowerment|CGAP

If the view is taken that Financial Inclusion is about enabling but not the end goal, then the key words in this quote are 'formal and informal income-generating opportunities'. Some may argue that women need to be financially included to take advantage of opportunities but if there is no need to be financially included why have an account? The focus therefore must be on developing income opportunities for women and Financial Inclusion will be the outcome.

A key factor is the balance of tasks within the family and if these have a bias towards males then there is a social/cultural task to change that balance. Financial Inclusion is a symptom and is unlikely to become the catalyst for change but could be an influencer. It is differently a gauge.

The low levels of inclusion for women reflect their low levels of participation in the economy. Is this a true statement?

There are claims that women will save more than males and specifically to cover the cost of education for their children. Is this true?

Is it difficult for women to borrow? Is money more easily available to men?

DOI: 10.4324/9781003471073-4

Statements are made that males are likely to be a higher credit risk. Females are less likely to default on a loan. Males are not so focused on the family's well-being and therefore do not save for education, etc. The macro view does not support this although at a micro level there will be cases of males not making the contribution to children's well-being.

The point is not whether one gender has an advantage over the other. The point must be whether individuals are achieving their full potential and how can Financial Inclusion contribute. All jurisdictions need both genders to contribute to their economic development and well-being.

The area of real concern must be as the payment systems begin to adopt digital methods there is a requirement for actors to investment in technology and develop a capability to use the technology. This potential is where woman maybe left behind if they do not have the resources or opportunity to invest in upskilling. The gap between the genders will blow out if this potential challenge is not addressed now. This is basically an education issue which can only be addressed through the development of well-funded programs.

A Macro View

The World Bank Findex data supports the view that women are less included, but across all income categories the difference is marginal, and it could be argued within the margin for error. But that is unlikely as it is constant. The data on financial accounts shows the gender gap increases for woman at the bottom of the socio-economic pyramid with 10% less low-income women having an account than males in the same category.

This is significant when comparing high-income woman where the difference in 2021 was just 1% for woman. Similarly, in terms of inactive accounts the gender difference for High-Income woman was again only 1% in 2021 but positive for males. In contrast, among low-income woman only 34% have an account compared to 44% of males. Inactive accounts are at the same level, that of 3% (Tables 4.1 and 4.2).

Table 4.1 does illustrate at the global level there is a minimal difference between the genders. However, the middle and low middle categories show that for both genders the inactive level is higher than the other categories. The table title suggests that an individual with two accounts could have both an active and inactive account. Possibly higher income woman may have multiple accounts (Table 4.3).

The same table above does not support females having a higher propensity to save. Males across all income categories are marginally better savers. It must be recognized this is a macro view and that not all individual countries will necessarily conform to this view. The World Bank data does show there are variances across countries where woman save more in various income categories.

TABLE 4.1 Financial Account Compared by Income and Gender

	Year	Female	Male	Difference
World	2011	47%	55%	8%
	2014	58%	65%	7%
	2017	65%	72%	7%
	2021	74%	78%	4%
Middle income	2021	70%	75%	5%
High income	2021	97%	96%	1%
Low income	2021	34%	44%	10%
Low middle income	2021	59%	65%	6%
Upper middle income	2021	82%	86%	4%

Source: World Bank Group, World Bank Group – Global Findex Database

TABLE 4.2 Inactive Accounts by Gender

	Year	Female	Male	Difference
World	2011	–	–	–
	2014	6%	6%	0%
	2017	9%	8%	1%
	2021	8%	6%	2%
Middle income	2021	11%	8%	3%
High income	2021	1%	0%	1%
Low income	2021	3%	3%	–%
Low middle income	2021	17%	13%	4%
Upper middle income	2021	3%	2%	1%

Source: World Bank Group, World Bank Group – Global Findex Database

TABLE 4.3 Savings by Gender

	Year	Female	Male	Difference
World	2011	–	–	–
	2014	54%	59%	5%
	2017	45%	52%	7%
	2021	47%	50%	3%
Middle income	2021	41%	44%	3%
High income	2021	75%	78%	3%
Low income	2021	43%	45%	2%
Low middle income	2021	32%	34%	2%
Upper middle income	2021	52%	56%	4%

Source: World Bank Group, World Bank Group – Global Findex Database

TABLE 4.4 Borrowed Money by Gender

	Year	Female	Male	Difference
World	2021	28%	31%	3%
Middle income	2021	21%	25%	4%
High income	2021	55%	57%	2%
Low income	2021	11%	14%	3%
Low middle income	2021	12%	14%	2%
Upper middle income	2021	35%	37%	2%

Source: World Bank Group, World Bank Group – Global Findex Database

TABLE 4.5 Digital Payment by Gender

	Year	Female	Male	Difference
World	2014	41%	47%	6%
	2017	48%	56%	8%
	2021	61%	68%	7%
Middle income	2021	53%	62%	9%
High income	2021	95%	94%	−1%
Low income	2021	31%	40%	9%
Low middle income	2021	32%	44%	12%
Upper middle income	2021	78%	83%	5%

Source: World Bank Group, World Bank Group – Global Findex Database

The World Bank data shows that women are more likely to save using a savings club or with somebody outside the family. This possibly supports the need to use a different saving service, so their male partner is unable to access the funds.

The ability for females to borrow is critical for them to have the ability to build a business. Funding may be required to start a business or to fund working capital during its development phases(s). Is it difficult for women to borrow? Is money more easily available to men? A savings record can be fundamental to securing a loan. A reflection of credit worthiness (Table 4.4).

Digital Payments

A question must be asked: will women be left behind in the digital world? The World Bank data supports this to be the case (Table 4.5).

At the top of the socio-economic pyramid, women are 1% higher than males (95% to 94%), indicating perhaps affordability and education; plus category of employment are both significant drivers in digital uptake. The lower-income categories woman are being left behind. This will have a negative impact if Financial Inclusion is closely aligned to digital affordability and education. Especially if digital inclusion has a dependency on having a smart phone. This may especially be the case for women where the data shows high-income women are more likely to receive or make a digital payment than lower income woman at ratio of 3 to 1.

Consideration must be the residential location of the lower-income categories. If a location is neither supported by mobile or electricity network coverage, then affordability and education becomes somewhat irrelevant for both genders.

Social Recognition

The author's view is that the general principles underpinning financial inclusion are applicable to both genders.

What are the social differences between males and females? – https://studybuff.com/how-does-meiosis-differ-in-males-female/ defines the roles of women as.

"The woman performs the role of wife, partner, organizer, administrator, director, re-creator, disburser, economist, mother, disciplinarian, teacher, health officer, artist and queen in the family at the same time." The roles of men as

"A Provider. Most men believe that being a good provider means supporting a family financially. …

A Protector. This means more than beating up the guy next door if he insults your wife. …

A Leader. …

A Teacher."

A payment system must adopt or conform to a societies gender roles. The payment system cannot be used to change the roles, as it will lead to failure in terms of take up of the services. The payment system can support social change if a conscious decision is made to ensure the user proposition is strong and supportive for all parties.

Bibliography

What are the social differences between males and females? By Perrine Juillion / January 26, 2020
World Bank Group, *Global Findex Database*, 2021.

5

MOBILE TECHNOLOGY DELIVERING SERVICES

MNOs looking to increase the activity levels of their subscribers (ARPU) and to reduce the churn (subscribers switching providers) viewed Financial Inclusion programs as strategically important and became committed to providing money transfer services. Consequently, Financial Inclusion programs have been based on mobile technology, not that there was in most circumstances a viable alternative. There were mutual benefits in MNOs delivering a service that satisfied the needs of all parties involved.

The starting service for Mobile Financial Inclusion programs was based on the delivery of remittances with a focus on increased reliability, trust, and lowering the cost for both the sender and recipient. The initial service was very basic but delivered immediate benefits and laid a foundation for future developments, which have been delivered especially in Kenya.

Several points need to be explored:

- What is the role and importance of the agency network?
- Are closed networks effective in delivering a competitive advantage and a customer service to a high standard?
- Should mobile payment networks be mandated to be part of the national payment system (NPS)?
- Is the need to upgrade rural networks to support broadband services being constrained by a case of a poor ROI, encouraging the MNOs to re-evaluate their future as a provider of Financial Inclusion programs?

As commercial businesses, MNOs must be focused on profit. Profit is derived by increasing market share and increasing ARPU. Simply, more subscribers generating more revenue through increasing usage of chargeable activity is

DOI: 10.4324/9781003471073-5

the foundation of success for an MNO. Can Financial Inclusion programs generate a profit contribution for MNOs?

The impact of smartphone technology (mobile broadband services) must also be considered. Will smartphones in effect enable Financial Inclusion services to be delivered by non-mobile network providers? Will mobile banking capture the market back from the MNOs? Will banks using the correspondent model and partnering with FinTech enterprises as per the India approach force MNOs to step back and possibly become a reseller of a service provided by a financial institution?

This chapter will examine the current role of MNOs in the delivery of Financial Inclusion programs and will ask is this to change in the future.

Agency Network

The two primary functions of an agent are the opening of accounts (mobile money or no-frills accounts) and the dispensing of cash. They also must be prepared to provide subscriber support.

The agency network for dispensing cash is very similar to that of a bank branch network. As the demand for cash declines, the need for a branch or agency network is also going to decline. Will these mobile money agency networks be around for the long term?

The business proposition for a merchant to become an agent is clear, especially if they are resellers of household supplies, etc. As recipients of money transfers are required to visit an agent/merchant to withdraw cash, they present the opportunity for the agent to sell merchandise. However, if the agency network experiences the problem of having insufficient cash then the business case for being an agent diminishes.

The chart below, sourced from the World Bank Global Findex Database 2021, illustrates the percentage of respondents that find the case of insufficient funds as a critical reason for not having an account and therefore effectively elect to be financially excluded (Table 5.1).

Further with the need for cash declining with the adoption of digital payments, the merchant's agency proposition will again diminish. The expectation

TABLE 5.1 No Account Because of Insufficient Funds

No Account because of Insufficient Funds - 2021

	Percentage without an account, age 15+
Upper middle income	58%
Middle income	61%
Lower middle income	62%
Low income	82%

Source: World Bank Group, World Bank Group – Global Findex Database

is that cash will be used by a percentage of the population across all the socio-economic layers of the pyramid for the foreseeable future. However, as the cash usage progressively diminishes, the agency business case diminishes. As digital payments across the counter increases, merchants are likely to lose interest in being an agent.

There will still be a need for agents as the trusted front office for mobile money, especially in respect to opening accounts and providing frontline account holder support. However, will the business case be strong enough for them to deliver this service without being able to either charge a fee or be renumerated by their mobile money (contracted) provider. At a point in time, support services will be delivered through an online help desk. However, this requires a means of communication.

Agent Technology Requirements

An agent must be connected to a communications network. In an ideal world that would be to an internet service, but a 2G mobile network can only offer narrowband services. Narrowband will constrain the capability of delivering extended services to account holders.

The level of the supporting technology platform is cost justified on the number of account holders being serviced. An advance technology platform will enable the merchant/agent to offer a more comprehensive set of services and generate a higher level of income. Foot traffic through a store (agent) will increase overall sales revenue.

Agents will also be affected by the increasing rollout of cash dispensers (ATMs/PBMs). This is not the case in Kenya. Kenyan ATM numbers are in a slow decline. However, in an article titled 'Mobile Money Payments Hit a Record of KES 8 Trillion' written by Leah Wakarima, it was reported that on the 8 August 2023, agents in the Kenyan Wall Street had increased to 317,983 over 298,272 in 2022.

The reduction in the number of ATMs is consistent with developed countries that are becoming increasingly cashless. Agent numbers also must reduce overtime as are bank branches in the developed economies.

Closed Networks vs Open Networks

Open or closed networks underpinned by interoperability was a debate between the payment system participants when electronic services such as ATMs and EFTPOS were first introduced. The advocates for open networks and interchange prevailed. For the mobile money providers, the situation could be argued to be different. In many jurisdictions two mobile network providers dominate the market, with a combined market share of more than 50%.

The banking sector in most jurisdictions is not dominated to the same extent by so few institutions. As an example, a country such as Australia there are four dominant banks but more than 89 other registered deposit takers. Many of the 93 own other institutions that are also deposit takers. Interchange between these institutions is critical to support the digital flow of money through the economy.

For mobile money participants to offer an open service, they need to support interbank (financial institution) settlement. Their options are to have an indirect arrangement with an existing payment participant or alternatively join the payments network as a fully participating (direct) member. There are costs and commitments associated with the two options and generally the decision on which approach to adopt relates to the volume and value of transactions the mobile provider will exchange with the other participating networks. These will be money transfer transactions initiated by the mobile money service account holders as well as transfers originating from an account holder of another network participant.

The underlying requirement is that open networks allow the financially included to be participants in the broader economy and not be restricted to boundaries of their provider. As the market size increases, the potential for small businesses and agricultural producers to increase their ARPU (revenue).

Regulating Mobile Money Providers and PSP (BC) to be NPS Participants

The indisputable point is that the banking sector is not well equipped due to their business model to service the needs of the financially excluded. Simply without the reengineering of their business model individual banks are not capable of servicing the lower levels of the socio-economic pyramid.

To service these lower levels the mobile operators or PSPs (India style banking correspondents - BCs) have demonstrated they do have the capability. A bank may consider there is strategic long-term value in partnering with a PSP/BC.

A Central Bank will look at the systemic risk of a mobile money provider, PSP, or BC. If the impact on the financial system of a particular provider failing is perceived to be significant, then that provider will be required to become a direct NPS participation. This will involve the provider holding an exchange settlement account and associated securities at the central bank. Size matters to Central Banks.

The expected approach is for mobile service providers or PSP/BC because of their limited-service offering, to only be an indirect participant. Connecting to the NPS through a bank and undertaking settlement through that bank. The key point from a financial inclusion perspective is the support for interchange across the socio-economic levels to ensure the full participation of all citizens of a jurisdiction in the economy. Therefore, regulating participation is essential. Stipulating the settlement regime to be adopted (direct or indirect) is of less importance to individual account holders.

Rural Broadband Services

The development status of a jurisdiction does not ensure all rural locations will be serviced by a broadband network. Isolation and a low population density impacts the ROI for any telecommunications provider. A negative ROI will translate to a minimal or no service.

It is more likely in a developed jurisdiction where rural incomes are higher, allowing citizens to address the telecommunications challenge through self-funding indirect connectivity to a broadband network. The author has seen this work effectively utilizing a microwave link through to a nearby town. However, this is not an option for lower-income actors from a cost perspective, especially where the terrain is not supportive.

Government or donor support is required.

The Current View and the Future Predictions

Two factors will have a major influence on the future of mobile money services, the market penetration of Smart Phones plus the rollout of mobile broadband. A rapid advancement of both will negatively impact mobile operators' mobile money services. This statement is based on the expectation that not only financial institutions, but also other service providers will be able to compete directly with MNOs. Competition will enter the market and is likely to deliver a more enriched service across an open platform. The question being whether MNOs will stay in the market or retreat to their core business, concentrating on the delivery of mobile core services. MNOs will continue to benefit from traffic across their networks.

The penetration of Smart Phones and the network capability are two factors that will determine the future direction of mobile financial services for the unbanked.

The following Table 5.2 shows the percentage of adults by region that have an account, financial institution and/or mobile, plus the percentage of those with a mobile account that use them more than twice a month.

The conclusions can be drawn from this data that the more prosperous regions are likely to have a high percentage of accounts with a low percentage being mobile. Sub-Saharan Africa shows a significant percentage of mobile money accounts at 33% but financial accounts are slightly higher at 37%. Latin America and Caribbean (LAC) is indicating a similar but smaller overlap situation of 54% of adults with a financial institution account and 22% with a mobile money account and the percentage with an account at 74%.

This situation is common across offer regions which may indicate that adult members of the same family might have different account types.

The following table illustrates the regional prospective (Table 5.2).

TABLE 5.2 Regional Prospective

Region		Account (% Age 15+)	Mobile Money Account (% Age 15+)	Financial Institution Account	Use a mobile Money Account Two or More Times a Month (% with a Mobile Money Account, Age 15+)	Used a Debit Card (% Age 15+)
East Asia & Pacific	2021	83%	5%	70%	3%	41%
Europe & Central Asia	2021	90%	7%	81%	2%	66%
Latin America & Caribbean	2021	74%	22%	54%	12%	37%
Middle East & North Africa	2021	53%	5%	47%		28%
North America	2021	95%	0%	94%		71%
Sub-Saharan Africa	2021	55%	33%	37%	22%	12%
Arab world	2021	40%	3%	37%		15%
Euro area	2021	99%	0%	95%		81%
South Asia	2021	69%	12%	68%		10%
World	2021	76%	10%	67%		35%

Source: World Bank Group, World Bank Group – Global Findex Database

A mix of accounts is significant as it indicates the situation in Kenya maybe more widespread where individuals have both account types which are used for different purposes. The data in the Kenya FinAccess Household Survey suggests one account is used for savings and the other for payments.

The percentage of those that use a debit card is included to demonstrate that having an account and debit card does not necessarily mean individuals will automatically be using digital payment channels. They may just be withdrawing money deposited into their account by another party, such as wages being withdrawn once month.

Proposition/Prediction

The prediction is that as smartphone penetration increases along with the networks progressively moving towards 100% 4G and/or 5G, the MNOs will lose dominance of the digital financial services sector. As previously stated, the development and introduction of mobile banking applications for smartphones has become common in the developed markets. As broadband mobile increasingly becomes available (and affordable) to the lower income market segments, supported by affordable handsets, MNOs may struggle to compete with those providers that have financial institution affiliation and are integrated with the National Payment System (NPS).

The key services offered by a mobile banking application are:

- 24-hour access to account information including transaction searches
- Money Transfer between an actor's own accounts
- Bill Payments
- Money Transfer to other actors (Direct Credits, Domestic and International money transfer)
- Loan Repayments
- Security and Fraud Alerts including temporary suspension of activity

In markets still supporting cheques, they can be deposited using the camera to capture an image.

The House of Commons Library – 29 Nov 2022 Statistics on Access to Cash, Bank Branches and ATMS provides the details on UK banking landscape.

Quoting Financial Lives Survey 2020, 46% of those who relied on cash were digitally excluded.

Payments by cash between 2015 and 2021 fell from 17 billion to 6 billion.

Using Office of National Statistics data, the total number of bank branches declined from 11,355 in 2012 to 6,305 in 2022, a fall of 44%.

This illustrated the impact of smartphones and mobile banking applications are having on a developed economy. The impact of smart phones on the emerging markets and those delivering banking services to the actors at the bottom of the socio-economic pyramid is unclear as handset affordability is a significant issue. There must be a point where the percentage of subscribers with basic/feature handsets falls to a level that maintaining support services is no longer feasible.

Key factors relate to affordability and digital literacy.

The ITU estimated in 2022 that in their category of LDC (least developed countries) 407 million individuals had access to the Internet.

The ITU state that the Internet annual growth rate is 5–10%. The LDC growth rate is more volatile being just under 40% in 2014 but dropping to 15% in 2022. The ratio of Urban/Rural between 2019 and 2022 narrowed from 2.5 to 1.9.

This drop is possibly indicating that those rural regions where delivery of an Internet service is less challenging the service coverage is improving. The mobile broadband subscribers for the LDC jurisdictions were reported by ITU as 42 per 100 subscribers where the world figure was 87 per 100 subscribers.

The averages do hide those countries where access to the Internet is still a major barrier to financial inclusion. The comparison between African and Asia/Pacific countries has a reported ration of 1 to 2. The ITU divides the 46 countries into for sub-categories and compares them to the world average. The top category is close to the world average, but the bottom category made up of African countries demonstrate the size of the gap that needs to be closed.

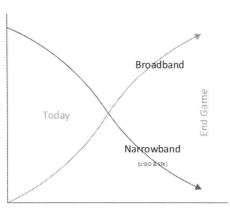

As Smartphones penetrate the market along with the rollout of 4/5G networks financial institutions (and their PSPs) will beginning to dominate the Financial Inclusion sector

Conversely the drop off of basic/feature phones will result in the decline of MNO's current hold on the Financial Inclusion sector

FIGURE 5.1   Broadband over Narrowband

Source: International Telecommunication Union

At the technology level Broadband over Narrowband delivers:

- Improved service levels (reliability) and coverage
- Improved user interface (mobile applications)
- Enhanced service offering

Narrowband services delivered over a 2G network are normally text based and often to the user are non-intuitive. USSD is also commonly used as the delivery channel.

MNOs Business Model

For emerging markets, the task of remitting funds especially by family members working away from home through informal channels can be slow, high risk, and costly. The mobile money services can be described as a digital delivery service or more specifically a money transfer service. As M-Pesa demonstrates, mobile money transfer services are successful if developed to meet the needs of the targeted population. Remembering the needs of the sender may be different to the needs of the recipient.

The MNO business model is a simple one. Dominate the subscriber base that is generating high ARPU. This objective can be delivered by a mobile money (transfer) service, at least in theory. However, a mobile money (transfer) service to be successful requires a significant commitment.

Impact of Smartphones and FinTech

It is without doubt that mobile addressed the remittance issues, especially in the domestic market. The technology of the basic/feature handsets is very rudimental in today's world. These handsets could be compared with the first ATMs taken to market in the 1980s. Both had/have a small screen, a limited keyboard, short on memory, and supported by a telecommunications network with limits. ATMS by using IoT technology have been transformed. Similarly mobile services for those further up the socio-economic pyramid have been transformed by Smartphones and by 3, 4 or 5G networks.

We are also seeing the Smart Feature phones, also referred to as hybrid phones, beginning to occupy the middle ground. The capabilities vary by type but wi-fi and mobile broadband can be an option. These phones are cheaper, using more dated technology.

Today's payment delivery channel providers of services such as mobile money and ATMs have embraced IoT. So, what will happen to the older technology? For ATMS the older devices have in effect disappeared, having been replaced or the service has been withdrawn. For mobile the shift is obviously towards smartphones, but the older technology is still entrenched in many markets.

Mobile Money Positives

Mobile money without debate can address the domestic remittance (money transfer) challenges. Recipients are receiving their money in a timely manner at a far lower cost with the security concerns minimized.

Mobile providers by launching mobile money services have been attributed with increasing employment opportunities and the income earnt through their agent networks.

Actors (account holders) have been delivered a secure repository for their savings.

Savings introduces the capacity for actors to borrow funds needed for an array of requirements.

Mobile money services are enabling actors to be move up the socioeconomic pyramid. Mobile money is the bases for delivering digital financial services, enabling sustained economic growth.

Mobile Money Weaknesses

The disappointment is that mobile money services have not saturated the targeted communities with digital payments to any significant degree. In Kenya, paying for every day expenses remains cash-dominant. The Kenya FinAccess Household Survey, 2021, highlights that 18.3% use cash exclusively while 80.6% use a combination of cash and non-cash payment methods. This means a very small percentage of actors (0.63%) never use cash. These figures show a significant percentage, in effect most of the population is comfortable with not using cash, but on a selective basis. This implies a need to build up the points of acceptance for non-cash payments and account holders will transition away from cash to digital, as is occurring in developed economies.

The deployment experiences of mobile money in several jurisdictions relating to building up usage was similar to EFTOS. Which comes first, rolling the service out to individual actors or building up points of acceptance, the merchant base? The strategy that worked for EFTOS in various jurisdictions was to build up the acceptance base within selective retail lines of business. Supermarkets and petrol outlets are two retail lines of business actors used regularly and if customers can rely on debit card acceptance there is no need to carry cash. This approach should work for mobile money.

Growing the Mobile Money Services Catchment

Initially the minimum requirement is to upgrade all 2G to 3G or even better to 4G or 5G. What is stopping this is the capital cost and the poor ROI.

Based on this view, there is a precedent for governments to initiate the establishment of a national utility with the task of delivering a national telecommunications infrastructure, inclusive of rural areas. Electricity grids are often owned by a government enterprise and service providers act as resellers delivering to the end consumer. Australian government funded and project managed the national broadband network.

Is there an opportunity for a jurisdiction's government to step up and fund the investment? Mobile operators could be enticed to become financial contributors in exchange for lower usage charges.

The banking/payments industry in many instances uses the phase, "Cooperate on Infrastructure, Compete on Service". This approach should be adopted by MNOs.

Refer to: Impact of Technology Advance on Existing and Future Services, Chapter 8.

As a country develops its national payment system regardless of the technology, regulations (or enhanced regulations) will be introduced to manage mobile money services. One of the regulations that should be introduced is that mobile money service providers must become a direct or indirect participant in the NPS. Participation of all deposit taking institutions allows the Central Bank to manage the systemic risk of the NPS.

Participation must be required to adhere with international standards covering messaging, security, AML, KYC, etc. This simply means interoperability compliance. If these requirements are not supported by the MNO's existing software, obviously undertaking an upgrade will be mandatory.

However, being a participant of the NPS is not all negative. Providing the potential to extend a mobile money service beyond the MNOs subscriber base does introduce the capability of decoupling the services from the MNO's own network allowing non-subscribers to become mobile money account holder. Subscribers of one MNO could become a mobile money account holder of a competitor's service. That is assuming the selected mobile money service uses a smartphone application.

In Kenya, we see that a percentage of the population has both a Financial Institution account and a Mobile Money account. This extends the actors options when making a payment by being able to split their funds across two services. One can be used for savings and the other for daily expenses.

If the MNO Mobile Money services are not mandated to become a participant in the NPS and the MNO elects to not be a participant (even if there is an option), their mobile money services are likely to become commercially unsustainable in the longer term. Competitive pressure will come from service providers who do participant in the NPS and offer an extended set of services. The mobile money participants offering an interoperable payment service will dominate.

Mobile Money Economy Positive Attribute to Covid-19

It is hard to imagine positives being derived by Covid-19 but perhaps the mobile money service did benefits; World Bank Global Findex 2021 reported on the following use case for 2021.

- Paid Utility Bill – 30%
- Sent Remittance – 35%
- Borrowed Money – 30%
- Mobile savings 39%

These levels are extremely positive and send a strong message to the mobile money providers. Interoperability with the banks is critical to drive up the activity rates and to move low-income individuals (families) up the socio-economic pyramid.

Bibliography

Central Bank of Keny, Kenya National Bureau of Statistics, Financial Sector Deepening Trust Kenya, 2021FinAccess Household Survey, 25 April 2023.

ITU, Facts and Figures: Focus on Least Developed Countries, 2022.The House of Commons Library –, Statistics on Access to Cash, Bank Branches sand ATMS, 29 November 2022.

Wakarima, Leah, Mobile Money Payments Hit a Record of KES 8 Trillion in 2022, 8 August 2023.

6

INTEGRATION WITH NATIONAL PAYMENT SYSTEM

Generally, Financial Inclusion programs have not been part of a country's overall NPS strategy or plans. India is an obvious exception.

Some may talk about the lack of interoperability between the NPS and the Financial Inclusion programs. This is largely because the developers of Financial Inclusion programs including the MNOs have built business cases focused on a narrow view of payments and perhaps of the economy.

Further, not all developing economies even have an NPS. The payment systems are not structured or networked so they can be managed as a single integrated entity. In several countries, no single entity has a holistic view of their NPS or been given the authority to develop such a view.

The Central Bank should be the organization working under directives from the central government which underpins its responsibility for the NPS. To quote a report published by the Bank for International Settlements January 2006, General Guidance for National Payment System Development:

"A central bank is a core contributor to national payment system development. It generally plays a variety of essential roles in the payment system. It is an operator, an overseer in core payment arrangements, a user of payment services and a catalyst for system reform. Through these roles, central banks acquire a broad perspective on the role of the payment system in the financial system and the economy, and expertise in specific payment systems. Central banks can thereby advice on payment and other financial system policies and act as an effective catalyst, together with private sector organizations, in initiating, promoting and contributing to payment system reforms."

DOI: 10.4324/9781003471073-6

This chapter provides guidelines for payment system development. There is recognition that there is a connection between economic growth and retail digital payment services that are safe and efficient, trusted and operate to facilitate low value fees.

The central bank must take a central role in the development of the national payment system focusing on the strategies necessary to improve the system's effectiveness to ensure it meets the needs of all the participants. A key part of this is to ensure the system is continuously evolving to take advantage of technological developments that deliver benefits in a timely way to meet the payment requirements of the domestic market. It is important not to be a leader but be a timely follower when the technology has proved its potential in terms of its value proposition.

The payment sector is a fertile target for the delivery of technology incapable of meeting expectations.

Central Bank Role in Payments Delivery

It is critical to note that from a payment processing prospective central banks are only interested in the settlement of payments between account holders of different financial institutions. Payments between account holders of the same institution do not invoke settlement processes.

The challenging step is to build out an NPS from the RTGS, involving the integration of existing disparate payment systems such as the mobile money services. The end goal is to establish a fully integrated service, supporting interoperability based on a regime of regulation and standards to minimize systemic risk. Delivering an efficient and secure NPS that satisfies the needs of the participants in the ecosystem, enabling social and economic development.

There is also the challenge for developing countries of building a payment system that is positioned to take advantage of the evolving services being developed in the more developed economies, based on proven technology advances and regulatory changes.

The most significant change taking place is the trend away from deferred to faster settlement. A shift away from end of day processing to continuous processing driven by the introduction of near real-time payment services, built on a new set of 'rails'. This change if adopted by the emerging economies should make their task easier. They can advance into the future.

Any new NPS must be developed to be future proofed.

National Payment System Conceptual View

The core of a national payment system revolves around the RTGS. This system manages payment instructions between participant financial institutions that are registered and have a settlement account often referred to as an Exchange Settlement Account held in the Central Bank's ESAS system. These accounts will be linked to the Bank's Central System Depository (CSD), where each participant's securities are recorded. If a participant bank is unable to settle their position at the end of a settlement window, a process is initiated to ensure it has the liquidity to continue to operate. This is when the securities may play a part.

The ESAS account is often referred to as a bank's current account at the central bank.

It is not unusual for a participant bank(s) to experience a short-term liquidity issue. In fact, the RTGS can experience what is referred to as grid-lock. This is where no bank can settle because one bank is waiting for a credit payment from another bank before it can settle with a third bank. RTGS systems must be designed to manage payment transactions queues to counter gridlock. Figure 6.1 provides the view of a NPS.

Faster Settlement System (FSS) type solutions are being developed to support the settlement of near real-time payments, which once processed successfully are irrevocable money transfer transactions. These transactions are similar to a money transfer in a mobile money system, however near real-time systems support interchange between financial institutions which introduces the need for the faster settlement process.

Refer to: Impact of Technology Advance on Existing and Future Services

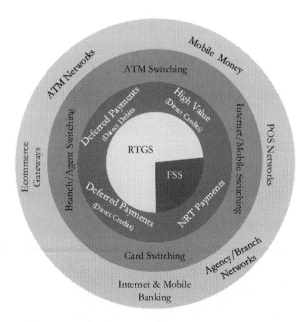

FIGURE 6.1   NPS Conceptual View

Non-repudiation (or irrevocable) is at the core of these systems. With immediate settlement, the recipient financial institution credits their customer's transaction account, making the funds available without any concern the payment may be reversed. Payments can be disputed; legal action may be initiated outside of the system. The recipient may be required to pay back the funds. This reversal will be a separate transaction. The payment system rule book must cover all such procedures.

Agency Network

Agency networks are similar to a branch network, they are typically independently owned. For competitive reasons, an agent will be aligned to only one financial institution (or banking correspondent). With no interoperability payments, where one of the parties is an account holder at another institution is not supported.

There is potential to develop this model, from their traditional role of 'cash out' for money transfers (remittances) to one of supporting inter-institutional transactions. Organizations such as Oxigen in India have taken agency networks to another level.

Delivery Channels

The delivery channels connect account holders to their bank. Generally, in this era of technological advancement all channels are at least partially digital. Even for agency and bank branches, the customer-facing staff will be assumed to be supported by a technology-based channel, delivering digitalized instructions/messages. Even cheques (or checks) are truncated into a digital form prior to being processed.

Network and Switching

The delivery channels have been developed and increasingly implemented to accept payment instructions from account holders of different banks. ATM networks once only serviced the account holders of the ATM owning bank. There are still ATM networks in many countries that are proprietary. They only accept cards issued by the ATM-owning financial institution. However, many ATMS and POS network owners are consortiums of financial institutions and therefore accept cards from a range of issuers. These networks require a transaction switch. The card schemes are in the same space, operating their own switches.

Payment Networks & Switches (Network Hubs) are the engine room of an NPS. Transactions do originate from a broad range of services, operated by financial institutions (banks) as well as PSPs (including mobile operators). It is feasible to have within an ecosystem multiple layers of switches. Visa and

MasterCard are payment networks, in effect a PSP who for many countries process both international and domestic transactions.

FEPs (Front End Processes)/switches support a gateway into financial institutions for the routing of transactions to their respective back-office destinations. They potentially can and do switch transactions that are referred to as 'not-on-us' out to the NPS. These are transactions a financial institution acquires, that are initiated by payment instrument holders of another institution.

The FINTech sector is focusing on APIs that fit into this space.

A financial institution's back office is often considered the domain of legacy (core banking) systems. It is not a component of the NPS but included for completeness.

As banking services/delivery channels, such an Internet and mobile accept instructions requesting the crediting of accounts held at multiple financial institutions, connectivity to an interbank switching capability is required.

With growth in the PSP sector, many delivery channels are starting to be owned and operated by non-financial institutions. Each requires a switching capability to connect to account holders' financial institutions. The card schemes belong in this space.

With switching, comes the need for settlement.

Clearing and Settlement Capability

Settlement can occur either as deferred or real-time. Traditionally it has been deferred often through the exchange of files over night after each participant's end of day. The end of business day net settlement position of the entire participant base is then calculated. In recent years, intraday settlement windows have been introduced allowing for intra-day net settlement. One middle east country where the author undertook an assignment for the Central Bank, supported six intraday settlements for their POS network. Ideally, today that would be replaced by an FSS where each transaction is settled in near real time.

An NRT channel can be supported by multiple intra-day settlement windows or by a faster settlement service where each payment is individually settled instantly. A faster settlement service, built into the NRT payment process utilizing participant reserve accounts managed by the central bank. Each transaction results in a credit and debit to the respective participant reserve accounts. The reserve accounts are funded from the participants ESAS accounts.

Clearing and Settlement Participants

Each institution that is an ESAS account holder is a clearing and settlement participant. Traditional participants have been commercial banks but with the development of the financial sector, participants can include:

- Ministries of Finance or Treasury Departments
- Investment Institutions

- Large Payment Service Providers
- Mobile Money Providers
- Large Commercial Enterprises

Organizations, such as mobile money providers, prepaid money providers, etc. may settle through a participant, normally a commercial bank who then carries the settlement risk. These providers are referred to as indirect participants.

Clearing houses cover the inter-bank processes for handling payments such as cheques, direct credits, and debits that are presented in bulk at the end of day (or in bulk for each settlement window). The batch processing of card transactions under the dual message protocol is in fact a clearing function. The risk of dishonouring a card transaction is mitigated by the provision and requirement for transactions that meet the criteria to be pre-authorized.

A cleared transaction is one that has been accepted by the two financial institutions. The debit will be honoured and therefore settled. Payments that fail to be cleared are dishonoured. Traditionally the clearing of a transaction may stretch across multiple days. FSS reduces this time to seconds or less.

RTGS is the interbank process for settling high value interbank transactions as well as deferred net settlement positions presented by the payment networks. Consideration for an NPS.

The following should be actioned as the first step in establishing an NPS:

- The normal practice is for the central bank to have the authority and responsibility for the regulations (operational) that govern the payment system. If this is not the case, then the government must empower the bank.
- A payment council must be established (if not already existing) made up of all the settlement institutions (direct participants) and the other major payment providers such as the PSPs and mobile money operators. The central bank should also be on the council and ideally chair all meetings.
- A payment council charter needs to be drafted with input from all council members. Penalties should be specified for cases of non-compliance.

Payments Council Charter

The council charter must cover the following elements:

- Purpose, objectives, milestones, and scope
- Participants, roles, responsibilities, and authority levels
- Governance and processes
- Resources and budget
- Advisory committees

Future NPS Architecture

Excluded

There is no justification in the open banking, real-time payment world for clearing houses supporting batch payments. If such clearing houses exist, they must be maintained until the transaction volume declines to a point where their existence cannot be justified. The end of day net deferred settlement positions must be processed through the RTGS.

Included

The traditional card payment schemes are supported by a set of rails that only facilitating a duel message protocol, ISO8583. For a transitional period, card scheme should consider migrating to ISO8583 single messaging, the 02XX series of messages. For future proofing supporting the ISO20022 message protocol will become necessary.

NRT payment, rails as implemented for the UK Faster Payment, and Australian NPP services are gaining global acceptance and should support both immediate and non-immediate (future dated or timed) payments. Non-immediate payments can be presented as a batch (bulk) but processed as single payment messages. NRT systems such as the Australian NPP support overlays, one of which has been designed to replace direct debits.

APIs supporting open banking is very much in its infancy and the NPS network needs to consider the likely impact and plan to support this method of connecting.

Subsidiary Networks and Delivery Channels

Financial institutions, mobile operators, and PSPs providing closed-loop services directly to citizens and businesses should not be part of the NPS. However, if open-loop services are being delivered to the customers of a select group of participant institutions then they should be connected to the NPS network for interchange and settlement purposes. Closed-loop services should not be sanctioned long term but in the NPS establishment phase, compromise may be required.

This implies that subsidiary networks and delivery channels must support the standard interfaces adopted by the NPS (ideally ISO20022). This should be encouraged if not regulated for closed loop services as well, where it is feasible. History suggests closed loop systems, when they reach a certain level of maturity will consider becoming an open loop service to generate further transaction growth. Non-compliance to a payment industry transaction standard is often a significant barrier for the transition from closed to open loop.

A challenge for emerging economies is that many have implemented mobile money services. These generally do not comply with standards. They were developed to support a feature phone user interface, based on USSD or text messaging. Two issues exist with these services; firstly, the effort and therefore cost incurred to transition from closed to open loop standards and secondly the feature phones have a short-term future.

The objective must be to implement a smart phone (IP) based services for the broader population, across the ecosystem utilizing the NRT or card rails, while phasing out the existing mobile money feature phone services as the usage declines. This may take a decade or three.

Focusing on Financial Inclusion

A Financial Inclusion payment system, supporting transitioning through the levels of inclusion must be built for efficiency reasons on two factors:

- A mobile network that is at a minimum 3G but preferably 4G or 5G
- A high smartphones market penetration (or smart feature phones as a lower cost option)

With these two factors, it is feasible to deliver a NRT payment service integrated into an NPS servicing all layers of the socio-economic pyramid.

It would not be impossible to integrate a legacy mobile money service using USSD or text channels to deliver transactions into the NRT system. In fact, the original Smart Money system (now PayMaya) did this to an extent. The issue is the scope of data that can be exchanged through the network and the security levels. A reasonable sophisticated gateway would need to be integrated into the NRT network.

Are payment cards to be excluded? No as there is always a requirement to allow account holders to access cash. This could be achieved through NFC (mobile handset) rather than by issuing a physical card. NFC could also be used at the point of sale to cover both purchases and cash out requests. However, there is a strong argument on whether card emulation is adopted or even needed. The challenge of card emulation is the need to support a separate switch and network.

Using QR Codes generated at the point of sale, a 'pay away' transaction can be initiated by the payer and sent by the NRT switch where the merchant's/agent's account is credited, and a message is returned to their mobile phone or POS device. The same approach for ATMs would also work with a message to the actor's bank requesting the crediting of the ATM owner's cash account, and for their ATM to dispense cash to the value of the payment.

In both cases the point of sale and ATM devices are required to generate QR Codes. This is not technically a challenge, but the payer needs to own and have in their possession a smartphone supporting a scanning application. It is not a frictionless process.

QR codes are likely to become more commonly used globally. There are various options available for using QR Codes.

The third alternative is for the merchant's device, mobile, or POS to generate a request to pay message sent to the NRT switch through their bank. The purchaser/payer on receiving the request to pay, is simply required to authorize the payment and payment message is returned through the system.

This approach will require the purchaser/payer to provide an account identifier to the merchant for the routing the request to pay message. This could be transferred via a QR Code.

As with every approach, the challenges are in the detail. Each of the approaches (and others) has the potential to be integrated into a network if only for a transitional period to allow participant institutions to upgrade their internal systems and networks. Exiting messaging standards, etc. would need to be enhanced to ensure the benefits of interoperability are delivered. The benefits are derived from having a single network and switching infrastructure supporting a broad scope of transactions. Volume delivers the ROI.

Payment Instruments/Form Factors (Including Mobile)

The basic question is how to identify the payer and payee.

If the payment instrument supports a card regardless of the form factor (plastic, mobile handset, fob, etc.), then the transaction messages are required to go down the card rails (network).

If the payment instrument supports direct account access such as Internet/Mobile payment services, then the near real-time rails (network) should be used.

The general view is that account holders have difficulty remembering their transaction account number(s), now referred to as their IBAN(s). Obviously if an individual is a customer of multiple institutions and/or have multiple accounts then they have multiple IBANs. The alternative is to use an alias that could be a mobile number, a token, or a name assigned by the account holder. Real-time payment systems generally are being developed to support aliases and mobile numbers. There being a recognized demand for supporting mobile-to-mobile money transfers. There is no reason for mobile to IBAN or IBAN to mobile not to be supported.

Card tokens have become well established in the mobile space and need to be considered.

NRT systems have been architected to support overlay processes that support mobile and aliases to their IBAN.

Who Builds the NPS

The central bank working in consultation with the payment council must take responsibility for the architecture of the NPS and then oversee its development.

The RTGS and faster settlement system (FSS) management of the exchange settlement accounts and other central banking activity needs to be the responsibility of the central bank, at the centre of the payment switch.

The central network switches or transaction hubs should be implemented by the NPS participants. It is a common practice for a consortium of financial institutions to be formed to implement and manage specific payment service switches. The larger PSP may see this as a commercial opportunity and set up centralized switching services for cards and/or NRT payments.

As the ecosystem matures with increasing citizen participation (as the banked population grows), the volume of electronic payments will increase, multiple switches will be supporting delivering multiple sets of rails. New players, especially PSPs, will enter the market and banks may even look to sell down their investment in the NPS.

There are three stipulations that must be adhered:

1 The centralized switches must service all participants. The fee structure should favour (within reason) those who have invested in a switch. Fees (or a discounted fee) enables a return for investors but fees should not be used as a barrier for newer or smaller entrants joining the NPS.
2 If there are multiple switches for one payment service (i.e., cards) then interchange between the switches must be supported.
3 The central bank through the payment council must retain oversight as the regulator.

Subsidiary Functions of NPS

The NPS must also support what can be referred to as subsidiary functions, but this does not mean they are less important.

Fraud and AML are two related areas where the NPS (Payment Council role), should maintain an across network view. The hubs/switches should all support a fraud and AML monitoring capability and where multiple switches are deployed there needs to be a sharing of case details. Neural technology should be considered.

Emerging Economies

In many emerging economies, an NPS may not exist as a coherent payment's platform although the World Bank and various NGOs are progressively addressing this core requirement.

For retail (or consumer) payments, it is not unusual in emerging economies for silos to exist. A silo will consist of a group of financial institutions, who are not direct competitors cooperating to deliver a payment interchange service exclusive to the group's transaction account holders. An example may be a group of regional credit unions supporting interchange between themselves but are not integrated with the NPS and therefore do not support interchange with the retail banking or mobile money services.

It is important for all financial institutions and payment service providers to be compliant with the national standards, so a holistic approach is developed. This will remove the major integration barriers. A national payment network can be established without the need for significant system redevelopment. A strategy to fully integrate all payment systems of the same type within an ecosystem needs to be agreed by all parties along with a supporting implementation plan.

From a strategic perspective payment system, participation should be classified in terms of layers or commonly referred to as tiers based on the services they deliver.

From a system perspective, the NPS framework is required to reflect a standard industry framework. This framework has the central bank and their RTGS system at the centre or at the top of the structure. The financial institutions are tiered with tier one comprising of those with an ESAS account and are referred to as the direct participants.

Tier two financial institution do not have an ESAS account and must settle through an account they have with their nominated settlement institution (participant). There are various variations to this relationship depending on the capability of the ESAS, such as a subsidiary ESAS account to a tier one institutions primary account.

It is also feasible to have tier three institutions, these may be PSPs, micro loan lenders, a credit union, etc. This tier can settle through either a tier 2 or 1 institution.

Near Real-Time Payments Network

NRT payment networks can be implemented for net settlement to be managed in the same traditional manner as ATMs, POS, etc. networks. Alternatively, FSS are being implemented, as is the case in Australia their NPP is supported by an FSS.

A financial Institution's FSS settlement accounts are updated in real-time to support payment non-repudiation and reducing the systemic risk.

If a settlement cannot be completed because the originating Tier 1 institution has insufficient funds in their FSS settlement account, the Central Bank must have a process in place to address this situation to ensure the service continues and account holder trust in the service is maintained. An account holder receiving a message declining a transaction, informing them that their bank has insufficient funds is likely to result in a lack of confidence that the financial system and a 'run on the financial institution' leading to the possible collapse of the national payment system. The process may involve the transfer of funds from the effected institutions ESAS account or from reserves which are held with the Central Bank. The Central Bank may lend funds (with interest payable plus a penalty) to the effected financial institution with the situation being addressed at the end of the current NPS settlement window.

The central banks must manage the systemic risk resulting from a NRT settlement failure. Refer NRT payments for a full coverage of a NRT systems.

Payment Service Providers (PSP)

Although payment service providers (PSPs) have been part of the payment landscape for several years if not decades, they have grown in number in recent years pushed along by the FINTech movement. In many developed markets, the monetary authorities and central banks have looked to open the payment ecosystem to third parties who can offer a broader change of services at a lower cost.

This has not been totally opposed by the banking industry as retail payment services have not necessarily been a large contributor to a bank's profits. Some banks do it very well and others poorly. Banks primary interest is to maintain the customer relationships, and many have extracted themselves from providing the delivery channels such as POS and ATM networks. However, they have developed Internet and mobile banking services to allow their customers to manage their own financial affairs and avoid the need to visit a branch. Customer support is increasingly being delivered through call centres.

The card industry, specifically or originally in the North America has used large PSP organizations for acquiring transactions from merchants. Global POS and ATM networks have either been acquired from the banks or established from scratch in both developed and emerging markets. The mobile and prepaid space has also been segmented with high PSP participation.

National Payment System and Mobile Money

It is critical for payment services established to support the financial inclusion market to be integrated into the NPS. This then allows the free movement of payments/money transfers between the social divisions in the most efficient manner (low cost, low risk, speedily).

The mobile money operators (and wallet account providers) are not normally a holder of a central bank exchange settlement account, so they need to have a relationship with a participant financial institution. This relationship will involve an account at the financial institution that is in effect a default settlement account and must be funded to ensure the financial institution is not carrying a risk. The normal practice and a licensing requirement for a mobile money operator is to hold their account holders' funds in a trust style account. This account should be held at the financial institution providing the settlement service.

Financial Inclusion Impact

The impact on the financial inclusion sector of being integrated into the NPS is they are not isolated or excluded.

Account holders are not in a situation where they can only transfer or received money from those in a similar situation to themselves. The full socio-economic marketplace is open to all regardless of their position on the hierarchy in respect to be able to conduct business (to be a participant).

Kenyan Payments Strategy

The Kenyan central bank National Payment Strategy (National-Payments-Strategy-2022–2025.pdf)(centralbank.go.ke) is an interest document that many countries, small or larger, economically developed, or developing should embrace with perhaps some modification.

Their Vision statement:

"A secure, fast, efficient, and collaborative payments system that supports financial inclusion and innovations that benefit Kenyans."

Of this vision there is only one word that should be challenged, innovations.

It could be argued that M-Pesa was innovative, attracting the world's attention. What was key to M-Pesa success, was the user proposition. Undoubtedly socio-economic and environmental elements supported the proposition. Are Kenyan's looking to repeat this success? The rule for countries such as Kenyan is to be a fast follower but not to be a pioneer. M-Pesa was a fast follower after the two Philippine mobile operators.

Their stated four key Strategic Objectives, are:

1 To support a payments system that meets the diverse needs of customers, especially with respect to financial inclusion and shared prosperity
2 To enhance the safety and security of the payments system through the adoption of relevant industry and global standards
3 To support an ecosystem that is anchored on collaboration that produces customer-centric and world leading innovations

4 To create a supportive policy, legal and regulatory framework that is robustly enforced across existing and emerging players in the payments ecosystem

The key learnings from their M-Pesa experience are expressed in the following quote:

> "A payments system can only contribute with a wider economic and social development, if customers find it relevant and applicable to their day-to-day payments needs. While being a subjective concept, usefulness is taken to mean that the payment needs of users are reliably met in a cost-effective manner."

To a large business or multinational company, usefulness is predominantly about security. For these users, usefulness is about having a guarantee that large payments will reach the right beneficiaries securely in order to enable these large entities to meet their contractual obligations with their customers or comply with AML/CFT requirements.

A final quote from the Kenyan Strategy that is key to delivering Financial Inclusion.

> "Payments are [an] integral part in the economy thus affordability and usefulness of the payment options in the market is critical. This will also boost financial inclusivity in the economy thus creating a robust platform for ease of exchange of value." – Bank

7

NEAR REAL TIME (NRT) PAYMENTS

Societies in general with the advancement of technology and its influence on individual lifestyles have developed an expectation that tasks that have historically taken time will now be performed immediately. This expectation is impacting businesses, increasing the demand for immediacy in the overall commercial process of buying or selling products and services.

This also applies for person-to-person funds transfers.

NRT payment platforms are being introduced in both developed and emerging economies, replacing the traditional ACH systems that were developed originally for paper-based payment instruments. ACH operations have in recent years been modified to support intra-day clearing and settlement, although traditionally they cleared and settled payments over night and only on business days.

NRT payment platforms, that may also be referred to as instant and faster, provide the opportunity for Financial Inclusion services to be integrated into a countries' NPS. Removing the barriers inherent with many closed loop mobile money and digital cash services.

Stimulation of the Economy

There is a view that a country's economy will grow if the velocity at which the funds circulate is increased to an optimal level. The goal of an NRT payment platform must be to extend the reach of digital money transfers and ideally reduce the dependency on cash, and in doing so reduce the latency in the payment system. Simply if a farmer or a fisherman is paid immediately on the sale and delivery of their produce, they can pay their workers and continue to fund and grow their business. It also enables them to build capital for the

DOI: 10.4324/9781003471073-7

expansion of their business in a timely manner. The requirement to source working capital externally is reduced.

All businesses regardless of size have a focus on their accounts receivable and the time it takes customers to pay.

Payment System for the Next 20 Years

United Kingdom payments' statistics clearly demonstrates the trend away from batch clearing, which is now in a pattern of negative growth in comparison to Faster Payment. Faster Payment growth is coming from multiple sources such as replacing cash and cheques as well as from the clearing houses.

The UK Faster Payment service has driven its acceptance though increases in the maximum transaction value, which is now set at £250,000, although individual participants are able to set lower limits.

The UK is undertaking a payment infrastructure rebuild referred to as the New Payment Architecture (NPA), where Faster Payments, BACs, and cheque processing will be integrated within a single platform. Migration to ISO20022 is an element of this architecture. This will be undertaken by an organization referred to as Pay.UK.

The NPA is not necessarily a completely new approach. There are software vendors delivering integrated payment platforms covering:

- Deferred Credits (batched)
- Deferred Debits (mandated)
- NRT Payments (credits)

These systems provide a platform for moving forward, where the constraints imposed by legacy technology can be removed from the payment system. The end of day will be replaced by continuance processing and simultaneous settlement. This means the approach of presenting batches of deferred payments will be replaced by the uploading of individual transactions, each with its own settlement date and time.

The payer will be able to specify the date and not before time for their payment to be processed and funds exchanged.

RTGS systems will continue primarily for participants to manage their exchange settlement accounts and reserve accounts. Very high value transactions will continue to be processed by the RTGS but expect these to diminish as the NRT maximum transaction value increases.

NRT Capability of Dominating Payments

It needs to be considered that new payment methods require a change in human behaviour, which translates into having a strong proposition covering convenience, cost, and ease of use.

Debit card use demonstrates that changing human behaviour is possible, over a long period. This is especially demonstrated by NFC. When introduced there was resistance primarily relating to security and the belief that proximity to a reader would result in unknowingly paying for somebody else's purchase. Covid-19 reinforced the proposition by removing the need to touch a device's pin pad and acceptance of the technology soared.

UK Finance in their paper, UK Payment 2019, have predicted that by 2024 debit cards transactions will account for 50% of all UK's payment transactions. If this occurs, the sustainability will depend on the introduction of enhanced and technology-based delivery additional services. This has substantially occurred.

NRT payments have demonstrated they are accepted as the method suitable for paying bills and as a replacement for cash in the one-off or p2p payment space. NRT unlike debit cards does not require the payee to have any technology as the process is initiated by the payer.

NRT Cross Broader

There will be a network established to support NRT cross border payments. SWIFT are working on a service with the title SWIFT Go. Their website states that this service will be a fast, highly secure, and competitively priced. This will enable SMEs and retail customers to initiate payments against their bank account from anywhere in the world. This has the potential to change the remittance services offered today.

A group of banks are currently piloting this service. What will be interesting is if financial institutions (or their Central Banks) integrate this service with their domestic NRT service. Participants extending their Internet banking and/ or mobile banking services so their customers have a single channel covering the full range of payment options to meet their money transfer requirements.

This type of payment service (cross border NRT) can support the introduction of a global digital currency where all international payments in such a currency are settled.

Basic Functions and Flow of an NRT Platform

For the illustration of the basic flow of a payment instruction, direct credit navigating a basic NRT platform refer to Figure 7.1.

Reasons for Implementing an NRT Payment Method – Across all levels of the socioeconomic pyramid (Figure 7.2).

Immediacy

With the advancement of technology and its influence on individual lifestyles, societies have developed an expectation that tasks that have historically taken time will now be performed immediately. This expectation is impacting businesses, increasing the demand for immediacy in the overall commercial process of buying or selling products and services.

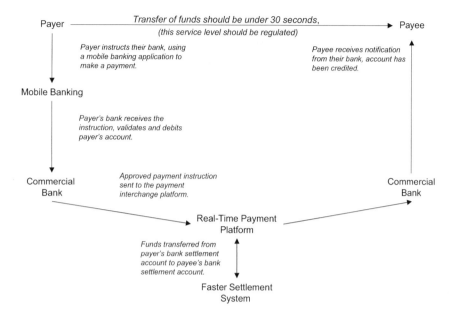

FIGURE 7.1 NRT basic flow

This also applies for person-to-person funds transfers.

Payer Control

This is a critical reason and is related to the payer having direct control over their funds with a degree of certainty. The alternative in many cases is to use a card, credit, or debit where the payment is initiated by the payee and although the payer's account is debited in real-time, the payee's receipt of payment is often delayed. Cards are also more open to fraud. Direct debit is another payment method where the feeling again is one of passing control to the payee.

Overlays

These are services that sit outside the NRT system but are integrated component of the platform. Developed either by a financial institution or by a third-party provider (e.g., FinTech). Overlays are normally integrated with the financial institutions' mobile/internet banking application. Osko in Australia is an example of an overlay that allows bank customers to initiate bill payments between participating banks and financial institutions.

The most common overlay supported for users is the registering of their mobile phone number and/or email address enabling it to be linked to their transaction bank account. If a user is not registered, the system will send a text or email message if a payment is received, requesting the user to register enabling the funds to be credited to their account. This only needs to be undertaken once.

This overlay may allow payers to use their mobile number or email address as a substitute for the account numbers.

Request-to-Pay (R2P)

The simplest use case for an R2P is a biller sending a client an invoice requesting payment. This could be a one-off payment, or a regular payment associated with utility companies and lending institutions. The request to pay is a non-financial transaction but contains sufficient data to enable acceptance by the NRT system for processing.

The R2P primary use case is to replace the traditional direct debit transactions where an account holder provides a business with a mandate to debit their account, often referred to as a pull payment. In effect, R2P turns direct debits upside down, so they become a push transaction where the account holder is fully in control.

The payment process can be automated where the payer is required through their financial institution's mobile banking application or Internet banking site to set up an authority to allow on receipt of a specific R2P for the financial institution to generate a direct credit, based on specified registered criteria. Examples of these criteria can be value range, day in the month and frequency. The account holder has the ability to suspend or cancel the authority at any time.

There is an upside for businesses in terms of receiving payments, assuming the criteria are satisfied in near real-time. There are likely to be fewer dishonours, possibly as the account holder is aware when the payment will be requested, and the credit generated. The traditional direct debit services can take two to three days to be processed.

Overlay Financial Inclusion Applicability

It could be argued that overlays are not appropriate for those at the bottom of the socio-economic pyramid who have little to no experience using either a mobile application or initiating payment instruction. This view is probably correct.

However, there must be opportunities to build overlays that are designed to assist those in this position to adapt to using financial services. Overlays with a user interface that is iterative to use, after minimal training enabling a digital payment to simply set up. Making this approach more convenient than paying with cash.

Bank Focused Solution

The term 'Bank Focused Solution' may imply a bank controlled or managed solution but should be viewed as a service compliant to payment industry standards and best practice that can be interconnected across all providers, banks, non-bank financial institutions, MMOs, PSPs, etc. In essence, this is the approach that India Reserve Bank has taken.

This implies:

- Subject to Central Bank governance
- Participants hold a Central Bank settlement account or participants are sponsored by a settlement account holder (indirect participant)
- System(s) compliance to messaging standards, i.e., ISO20022
- Compliance to PSD2/3 regulations, especially relating to security

With this approach, the system can and should become all inclusive. The economic status of an account holder may determine what services are delivered based on their need but should not limit their ability to transact with an actor holding a different status. This is vital to achieve broad-based economic development through commercial activity. The payment system must not discriminate based on an individual's financial status. Cash does not.

Actors (businesses and individuals) should be able to transition up through the services or pyramid levels with the minimum of disruption. Financial Inclusion is a matter of degrees until full inclusion is achieved.

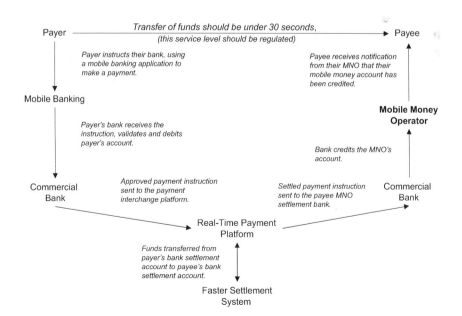

FIGURE 7.2 Navigating NRT

NRT Integration with Mobile Money

It is critical for all established payment services supporting the financial excluded market to be integrated into the NPS. This then allows the free movement of payments/money transfers between the social divisions in the most efficient manner (low cost, low risk, speedily).

The following chart illustrates a payment instruction originating from a financial institution's customer using a mobile banking service to credit a mobile money account held by an MNO.

User Directory

Typically, NRT payment services require users to download an app onto their handset, supplied by their financial institution. Alternatively, or as well as, each financial institution's website should support access through to their NRT service. This process must involves a service registration managed by the financial institution involving both customer identification and authentication. The registration processes typically involve linking a mobile phone to an account or accounts held by the same financial institution.

This is normally a binary relationship so an actor with multiple accounts at more than one institution is required to register with each and download each institutions mobile application. There is an opportunity for a FinTech/PSP organization to address this inconvenience. This maybe a use case for open banking.

Mobile subscribers who do not have an account with any category of financial institution should be able to open an account at their institution of choice or a mobile money account if offered by their MNO. Logic would suggest a no-frills or mobile money account would be the entry point for unbanked actors to become banked.

In sending a payment to another party, that party's identification can be based on several options. This requires the NRT platform to support a proxy overlay that links mobile numbers, email addresses, etc. to financial institution account numbers. There is also the requirement to support mobile money to mobile money accounts held at other MNOs.

For payment to business or between businesses either the recipients account number could be used or the recipients' financial institution my issue a business bill payment identification (code). The identification would be issued when a business registers. Registration would not be required if the account number is used. Similar account numbers if used for P2P then the recipient does not need to be registered.

Typically, businesses will need a payer reference number to be entered when initiating the payment transaction. This is so the business (payee) on receipt of the payment can identify the payer. In addition, an invoice number may also be required if payments are off set against a specific invoice.

NRT Governance

For any payment service to be successful, trust is extremely import. As we can see in the various financial inclusion surveys, the lack of trust is a critical reason for not using a payment service.

The critical advantage and issue with a NRT payment service is that funds are transferred immediately and are irrevocable (services do not support reversals once a transaction is completed). A dispute process must be established. NRT systems are a direct substitute for cash. Generally, the value of a transfer is restricted by a maximum limit. Restrictions on the maximum amount that can be debited within a period (day, week and/or month) should be set for the individual account holder and/or by account type specified by the financial institution.

The Rule Book

Governance for each payment system should be based on a 'rule book' covering all participants and service providers.

Rule Books are service specific but typically, they should cover:

Participant

- Membership

  - Identification
  - Suspension/Expulsion
  - Withdrawal

- Responsibility to Maintain Liquidity
- Technical Requirements & Operations

  - Network Connectivity
  - System Availability
  - PKI Management

- Customer Notifications

Transaction Processing

- Transactions Supported
- Cancellation
- Declines/Rejections
- Response Times

Payment Settlement & Finality
Dispute Management
Non-Payment Message Processes

Message Types

• Priority

Security Controls

• Separation of Domains
• Encryption of Messages
• PKI Security
• Access Controls

Rule book should also cover:

• Testing and Certification
• Change Management
• D & R Procedures
• Fees and Charges
• Obligation to Law

Participants when they sign up to the service must commit to conducting their service in compliance with the rules. Failure to do should attracting a penalty.

Integrating Mobile Money Services

There is no reason why an NRT payment service cannot support user access from a basic or feature phones. There would be compromises due to the inferior user interface and the security limitations. This would be translated to a minimum transaction set and lower maximum transaction values. A SIM Tool Kit application with a simple user interface is advisable not only because of the user interface but because basic security elements could be utilized.

The transactions being delivered by an existing mobile money service covering transaction types P2P, bill payment, and balance enquiry can still be supported. The limitations would apply to ATM cash withdrawal and merchant purchases where NFC capability may be used to support the device-to-device dialogue. Undertaking transaction searches and accessing other account details beyond a balance enquire may be a challenge for basic and feature handset.

Technical Interface

An integration module would need to be developed to translate USSD or SMS messages off the MMOs network to a format that can be passed through the NRT platform. This would only be needed to support not-on-us transactions originating from a basic/feature phone where the payment is to an actor with an account at financial institution or another MMO. Similarly, there would need to be the capability for the platform to transfer a credit payment to the recipient's (payee) MNO's mobile money service, for their mobile money account to be credited. MMO systems support money transfers between their own account holders.

An alternative if a mobile money service is not an NPS participant (not direct but indirect) is to implement a connection to their NPS participating financial institution. The participating financial institution then forwards the transaction messages to the NRT payment platform and becomes the settlement institution for the MMO. However, this would not be desirable especially if the MMO is generating a high level of transactions.

The issue of ISO20022 compliance will arise as mobile money systems cannot be expected to support this standard which is now commonly supported by the available NRT systems. Integration will require a gateway solution that translate the messages. Not always an easy task.

MMO Business Strategy

The MMO strategy should support two services. Firstly, connect their existing mobile money subscribers through the integration of their existing service with the NRT platform to support P2P payments to and from account holders of other MMOs and financial institutions.

Secondly, utilizing a smartphone app for subscribers connecting via a 3G, 4G or 5G network. Over a period of five to ten years, the 2G connected subscribers will have been transitioned to smartphone technology or their service will be discontinued. For subscribers the migration should only involve downloading the app and registering their change of status.

There will be a transition period where an MMO is required to support both the current service and the Smartphone/IP based service as no upgrade is going to be instant and cover the total subscriber base.

MMOs have a third option. Just develop a strategy to close their existing services and concentrate on other revenue sources such as those linked to mobile data. To minimize the disruption this option would create, the account holders should be transitioned to a comparable service, or the existing service be taken over by a PSP, banking correspondent type organization or even a financial institution.

8

IMPACT OF TECHNOLOGY ADVANCES ON EXISTING AND FUTURE SERVICES

Many financial inclusions programs were developed prior to the establishment of the 'Internet of Things' or more specifically smart phones. The now dominance of smartphones changes the fundamentals of financial inclusion solutions.

In 2024, you would have built a mobile payment service quite differently to what was built in 2000.

The level of penetration of 3 & 4G networks in developing economies is covered in the chapter 'Current View and the Future Predictions'. Many areas (especially rural) are still being serviced by 2G networks. This drastically restricts the payment service that can be delivered with the user interface at best being described as primitive.

This chapter, at a high level, will examine the technology options for building a 2022-and-beyond service.

Mobile Networks and IoT

The author has been involved with the development of the first recognized mobile money service, Smart Money by Smart Communications in the Philippines, in 2000. The author refers to these earlier services as being based on what is now legacy technology. In the same way as the early back-office banking systems have been referred to as legacy systems. This is just the fate of all systems built using technology available at the time, but now two decades on technology offers so many more alternatives.

The issue now with Mobile Money services is the cost of upgrading, especially for those services that have had minimal success. The financial

DOI: 10.4324/9781003471073-8

justification to support an upgrade is negative. There are three elements to an upgrade:

The upgrading of the network from 2G to at least 3G but preferably to 4G.

The redevelopment of the systems to take advantage of smartphone technology, although at a basic level it amounts to rearchitecting the user interface.

Transitioning the customer base into the LoT world where there are availability restrictions.

The theoretical business case being that by upgrading capability and capacity to support smartphone subscriber activity (inclusive of financial services) will generate additional revenue, necessarily to achieve an acceptable ROI. This revenue increase being derived from mobile data. The mobile operator battleground today is that of content, which translates to data.

A key question is there enough demand and more importantly wealth in the lower socio-economic communities to generate the revenue from added value data related services. At best, the proposition is most likely to be only financially marginal.

The key alternative question is whether the services delivered today to the less populated and lower income geographies will be discontinued especially if 2G technology is allowed to be phased out. Noting the business case to support an aging network will increase over time.

Low populated geographies are often made up of rugged terrain with poor infrastructure such as access roads and minimal power supply. These are the necessary prerequisites for the delivery of a highly reliable network. Maintaining a network is as critical as establishing it initially.

Whatever the case, it can be argued a two-tiered financial inclusion sector has emerged at least for a period.

An article written by Leon Perlman and Michael Wechsler, titled, 'Mobile Coverage and its Impact on Digital Services', 17 May 2019, provides an insight into the challenges facing financial inclusion programs and offers options.

Perlman and Wechsler state,

"Findings from our research suggest that provision of mobile coverage in rural areas in developing countries does not provide an adequate return on investment for MMOs and that in many cases because of expansion costs and costs to upgrade from 2G to 3G and higher services, 2G services will be the only technology provided to rural areas by individual MMOs."

If we accept maintaining 2G networks is not a long-term proposition, then there is a time limit for these services to either be upgraded or be closed.

Alternative Technology

Perlman and Wechsler in their paper touch on evolving innovations to replace the existing network of towers. These innovations may be used in emergencies, such as natural disasters. Alternatively, other approaches may prove to be a more permanent solution for especially remote populations. These innovations cover micro-satellites, Google's Project Loon's air balloons and AT&T's drone system (called the 'COW in the Sky').

Project Loon was looking particularly interesting. To quote from the website, "Billions of people around the world are still without internet access. Loon is a network of balloons traveling on the edge of space, delivering connectivity to people in unserved and underserved communities around the world."

Loon closed in 2021, but hopefully all is not lost.

Change of Direction

In many countries MMOs have traditionally built their own networks, especially in areas of high population density. A few to improve their ROI have moved to commercialize their excess network capacity. There are the normal investment regimes that can be used to fund the development of networks, but the revenue flow must be supportive to carry the cost and deliver a ROI on the funds invested.

As previously mentioned, the banking industry users the phrase; "cooperate on infrastructure, compete on service". The MMOs need to consider this approach. Build jointly, comprehensive networks with a broad coverage and then develop individually product offerings based on a competitive pricing regime, etc.

Similarly, the NGOs, development banks, GSM, CGAP, GPFI, etc. rather than injecting funds into the development of financial inclusion services, an alternative is to target their funding at development of the infrastructure, i.e., 4G or 5G networks. A business model would still need to be developed to support the ongoing management for owners and operators, especially focusing on maintenance and ongoing network development. This is potentially where governments could provide support.

With 4G and possibly 5G networks owned and operated by third parties, the MMOs and other service providers can deliver their services out to the hard-to-reach rural communities. IoT-based services can be developed supporting a more intuitive user interface with the assurance of a very high level of availability.

There is an opportunity here for FinTech businesses cooperating with MMOs and PSPs to deliver specific innovated services to the underserved communities. These services as mentioned above do not need to be solely payment services but services that are based on enriched content and are of value to the subscriber base, at a low cost. Value added services to a financial inclusion service.

The only remaining challenge is to build handsets at an affordable price for the financially excluded. We are seeing this happen, as smartphones become increasingly a commodity and with the introduction of smart feature handsets.

More Importantly

A key aspect of building and delivery mobile networks that reach out to all is the opening of commercial opportunities. Standing on a beach in the Maldives, the author watched as tuna fishermen unloaded their catch while the boat owner was on his mobile phone enquiring about the prices being paid for such fish. The owner needed to decide whether to send his catch to a cannery, to the market or to dry the tuna himself. This was a simple example of the fishing boat owner using mobile technology to manage his business. This was all happening before any payment was processed. A clear indication payment is an enabler of commerce, but payments are not the creator of commercial opportunities. The mobile network delivers a boarder capability than financial inclusion; importantly it delivers business inclusion (payment is only an element).

Ideally on making a decision and delivering the tuna, the boat owner would receive payment immediately and then be able to pay his fishermen immediately.

9

KENYA AND INDIA, OPPOSING APPROACHES

Kenya and India offer two leading examples of Financial Inclusion based on their opposing approaches. Kenya's approach was based on a business opportunity that was recognized and driven by a mobile operator, whereas the Indian approach was based on a strategy to develop an inclusive national ecosystem that enables those at the lower levels of the socio-economic pyramid to migrate upwards.

Both approaches are more widely based than simply targeting the unbanked as they are inclusive of the total community with many individuals using services delivered by alternative providers. A key question is not whether they have been historically successful as the Kenya approach has been, whereas the Indian approach has yet to each maturity, but which one provides the best strategy for a developing economy.

Kenya Provides a Template

Kenya is one of the outstanding success stories in the drive for Financial Inclusion. This position was delivered essentially by the M-Pesa service, which started as a money transfer service (remittances).

The World Bank Global Findex Database 2021 informs us that in 2021 79% of Kenyan Adults had an account with 1% of them being inactive. This was made up with 51% of the adult population having a financial institution account and 69% having a mobile money account. This implies that approximately 40% of the population has both types of accounts. In 2021 where 38% had more than one account. Inactive accounts are low, ranging from 3% to 1% over the same period.

DOI: 10.4324/9781003471073-9

In looking to understand the status of this country's Financial Inclusion, the 2021 FinAccess Household Survey, available at https://www.knbs. or.ke/publications/, is recommended as the starting place. This survey has been conducted for each of the last seven years, 2009/2009/2013/2016 & 2019.

The focus is based on the goal to move payments (transfer of money) more efficiently and effectively through the economy by the digitization of money, enabling economic growth. There is no argument that digital payments (or money transfers) must dominate the ecosystem for Financial Inclusion goals to be achieved.

The percentage of actors in Kenya classified as participants in both the mobile money and financial institution categories as highlighted above is approximately 40%. It could be argued that these actors have an excellent understanding of the financial services being offered and are using services that most appropriately fulfil their needs. Alternatively, these simply are actors moving from informal to formal and have not completed the transition. Such actors can be expected to eventually close their mobile accounts once they are comfortable the formal sector can satisfy all their needs.

This situation may also reflect actors transitioning up the socio-economic pyramid resulting from building financial stability through their ability to improve their income earning capacity.

It is important to state the formal category covers both the Formal Prudential and Formal Non-Prudential Financial service providers and, in some cases, covering mobile money operators.

Assessment

The following analysis of Kenya will leave the impression that the country has progressed significantly in terms of Financial Inclusion, especially if you measure progress by the percentage of adults who have a financial account. The downside is the usage levels show there is still a considerable amount of scope to improve the economic and social outcomes.

Cash is still having a strong foothold in the agricultural and retail sectors of the economy. This could be due to the face-to-face nature of the client/customer relationship. There is as expected a usage/acceptance gap between the highest and lowest income segments of the population. The point is that Kenya has been able to build strong acceptance of digital payment methods, and this is likely to be extended across all sectors of the economy.

Education and wealth are also factors that determine if a citizen is financially included or not.

Banking Sector Benefiting from Mobile Money Success

Of interest is the increase in adult actors who have more than one account. This raises the question whether the banking sector is benefiting indirectly by the growth in mobile money. Is mobile money the entry point for actors to become fully committed to financial inclusion?

With nearly 79% of Kenyans having one type of account, half of those will have a mobile money account plus a traditional bank account and/or informal account.

To put this into perspective, with a population of 33 ml adults, 6.9 ml do not have any kind of account, but 9.8 million have potentially two accounts. This figure would be reduced if there are several adults having more than two accounts. The evidence suggests that the mobile money accounts are used primarily for money transfer. These accounts are also used more for savings (37%) rather than financial institution accounts (21%). Note also 2021 31% saved money using at a savings club or somebody outside the family.

This does not imply that more value is in the mobile money accounts. Cash dominates everyday payments in Kenya, and funds designated as savings maybe held for only a short period until converted into cash and spent. The World Bank data also covers were adults store money. For 2021, the numbers are: financial institution accounts 29%, mobile money accounts 51%, and 63% store money in both types of accounts.

The Kenya financial participating institutions offer a broad range of financial accounts. These being:

- Traditional Bank Accounts
- Mobile Bank Accounts
- Mobile Money Accounts
- Micro-Finance Accounts
- Saving and Credit Co-operative Accounts
- Informal Accounts

In 2011, the World Bank reported that 42% of the population held an account. This indicator of Financial Inclusion in 2021, showed that 79% of Kenyans who were15+ years of age, had an account. The numbers also point to 40% having more than one type of account with financial institution accounts at 51% and mobile money accounts at 69%. Approximately 21% of the adult population remain financially excluded.

The critical question is whether these accounts are being used. The need for multiple account types across different categories of providers is a further point of interest. In a developed economy, actors will have multiple accounts with the same financial institution and across institutions. For Kenya, is this a sign of a maturing Financial Inclusion ecosystem?

Excluded to Formal Banking

The World Bank data tells us that in 2011, 58% of the Kenya did not have an account. This percentage dropped during 2021 by 37% to 21%.

The FinAccess provides an insight into the Kenya payment system success as well as challenging the existing views. There are several observations that can be made based on the growth in accounts and perhaps more interesting on their classification.

As a general statement, the Covid-19 situation is expected to have impacted the 2021 statistics negatively, especially for the younger actors being included in the survey for the first time.

Access by Age Not Equal

What these figures indicate is the middle age groups are more active in the economy and therefore have a need to initiate and receive payments/money transfers. The technology associated with Financial Inclusion is not a barrier for this group.

Lack of Education a Barrier

The expectation is that lower educated members of society are likely to rank lower in terms of being financially included. For Kenya is this the case and do they have a bias towards mobile money. The World Bank Findex data can assist in answering this question (Table 9.1).

The table supports the hypothesis that being education is a key factor with those having a secondary education being significantly above the adult population. Those individuals with only a primary education may have a bias towards mobile but not significantly different to those with a secondary education. Secondary educated actors are more likely to be account holders of both categories (Table 9.1).

Table 9.2 also supports the hypothesis that education influences the take-up of technology. The financial institutions moving to offer mobile banking services must recognize this as a factor.

Urban vs Rural

Table 9.3 below for Kenya shows a predictable view with the urban adult residents showing are high percentage of both types of accounts. As previously stated, there is a high percentage of actors with both types of accounts. Of the urban actors possibly 50 percentage are most likely to have both. The take-up by the rural residents with an account is possibly higher than

TABLE 9.1 Education Impact on Financial Inclusion

	Account	Financial Institution	Mobile
All adults (age 15+)	79%	51%	69%
Primary education	61%	32%	50%
Secondary education	88%	60%	78%

Source: World Bank Group, World Bank Group – Global Findex Database

TABLE 9.2 Digital Payments and Access

	Made a Digital Payment	Mobile or Internet to Access an Account
All adults (age 15+)	78%	72%
Primary education	56%	55%
Secondary education	86%	84%

Source: World Bank Group, World Bank Group – Global Findex Database

TABLE 9.3 Urban/Rural Comparison

	Urban	Rural
Account	89%	75%
Financial institution	62%	46%
Mobile money	79%	64%
Credit card	8%	6%
Debit card	31%	19%
Made digital payment	85%	72%
Received digital payment	62%	55%

Source: World Bank Group, World Bank Group – Global Findex Database

expected, reflecting the broad base coverage of mobile money. Rural residents have a significant dependency on financial institutions; however mobile is dominant (Table 9.3).

Credit cards are not widely issued. Debit cards are also not as high as would be expected. The issuance of debit cards by financial institution to their account holders is obviously not a default practice. This maybe because of the lack of demand driven by a low number of points of acceptance. If the merchant base has a preference to accept cash rather and use an EFTPOS payment service then debit card acceptance will be low.

The number used in either making or receiving a digital payment is significant. This indicates a willingness to use the Internet or mobile services to pay bills and remit funds.

Livelihood

The need for a bank account and one held by a formal institution is illustrated by the following breakdown. The table links the need for a bank account to the sector of the economy an actor is receiving their income (Table 9.4).

Table indicates a stronger proposition exists for those receiving wages to hold a bank or mobile account. A key factor is the low percentage either receiving a wage or a government pension in cash. However, a third is receiving their earnings from agriculture are doing so in cash.

The percentage in the rural sector with financial institution or mobile money accounts suggests this should not be the case. The rural (agricultural) business model may need to be incentivized to change. May even be a tax evasion issue involved.

Wealth Quintiles

Table 9.5 confirms the expectation that the percentage of actors in the high-income category will hold an account. However, the 67% of the poorest or the lower income 40% do have an account. This poorest category is also making or receiving digital payments. The gap between the richest and poorest categories is however significant in the 20% range (Table 9.5).

TABLE 9.4 Bank Account to Income Sector

	Percentage of Adult Population	Financial Institution	Mobile Money	Cash
Received wages	30%	18%	13%	5%
Sale of agricultural products	30%	7%	16%	10%
Government transfer or pension	13%	6%	5%	1%
Domestic remittances	54%	41%		9%

Source: World Bank Group, World Bank Group – Global Findex Database

TABLE 9.5 Richest/Poorest Comparison

	Account, Income, Poorest 40%	Account, Income, Richest 60%
Account	67%	87%
Financial institution	36%	61%
Mobile money account	56%	77%
Debit card	11%	30%
Made digital payment	65%	83%
Received digital payment	44%	65%

Source: World Bank Group, World Bank Group – Global Findex Database

What Does This Really Mean?

Those actors with an account have increased from 42% in 2011 to 79% in 2021 with an inactive level at 1%.

There may be a legitimate need to have both a mobile account and a bank account. Had mobile money services not only driven up the acceptance for its own services, it must have given a boost to the number of account holders in the financial institution sectors. This could be distorting the statistics. The World Bank Global Survey for 2021 states that Kenya's banked is 51% financial institution accounts and 69% mobile accounts. A significant percentage of actors must have an account in both financial sectors.

This may indicate that one type is preferred as an institution for savings while the other is preferred for holding the funds to cover everyday spending, a 'cookie jar' approach to personnel financial management. This may also reflect a trust situation where banks are considered to represent a lower longer-term risk than mobile money providers.

The learnings are that:

- Urban dwellers are more likely to be financially included.
- Livelihood is not a significant factor unless an actor is in the dependent category.
- Wealth is not a major differentiator unless an actor is in the lower income category.
- Those without a secondary education are less likely to be excluded, at 84%.
- Age can also be a factor for those at the two extremes of the range. The World Bank Findex database does not provide an insight.
- It should also be noted that Kenya on the Country Index table scores 3.90 (refer to Chapter XX). Against the other countries, this places Kenyan on the upside of the mid-point at position 51. This implies Kenya has a broader reach of services than developed countries although not necessarily a higher frequency of use.

Level of Cash Usage

Comparing Kenya to the World Bank categories of the 'World' and 'Developing' categories is a high performer. The only payment category that has the potential to be addressed is agricultural payments. A third of the actors have received cash agricultural payments (Tables 9.6 and 9.7).

Regarding digital payments, the table above illustrates that Kenya is ahead of the world average. These statistics indicate that for Kenyans mobile money is the preferred money transfer channel, where funds are transferred within Kenya. But it is not as dominant as expected. With cash usage is only 4–5% lower. So how can this situation be changed?

TABLE 9.6 Cash Usage Kenya/World/Developing Economies

	Kenya	World	Developing
Received wages: in cash only	17%	20%	26%
Received government transfer or pension: in cash only	4%	3%	3%
Made a utility payment: using cash only	10%	32%	41%
Sent or received domestic remittances: in person and in cash only	15%	N/A	19%
Received payments for agricultural products: in cash only	34%	N/A	61%

Source: World Bank Group, World Bank Group – Global Findex Database

TABLE 9.7 Digital Payments Kenya/World Comparison

	Kenya	World	Developing
Made a digital payment	76%	59%	51%
Received digital payments	57%	43%	36%
Used a mobile phone or the internet to pay bills	45%	34%	29%
Used a mobile phone or the internet to send money	69%	35%	33%
Made a digital in-store merchant payment: using a mobile phone (% age 15+)	37%	32%	32%

Source: World Bank Group, World Bank Group – Global Findex Database

1 Point of sale payment technology must be promoted by incentivizing merchants to accept digital payments. Potentially this could be achieved through a mobile app utilizing NFC rather than the introduction of a physical payment card. This does carry a cost of enabling merchants but there are alternative and innovative technology solutions available.

   Example of an alternative approach is to use QR codes.
2 Direct credits through an NRT service (which is fundamentally mobile P2P) can be used for a range of payments.
3 Paying monthly bills digitally must be promoted by the business sector, specifically but not exclusively utility companies. These bills are normally regular with a constant payment value and due date. Consideration should be given to introducing direct debits. Direct debits do require the payers to be able to ensure funds to be available in their accounts. However direct debit payment methods do introduce a level of complexity that those at the bottom of the financially inclusion pyramid may struggle to accept because of the need for trust in the process. The issuance of a notification prior to initiating the payment request can address the trust factor.

4 With the introduction of near time payments there are alternative approaches
to the traditional mandated direct debit that potentially could be more
acceptable to account holders. These are based on the 'Request to Pay
(R2P)'. R2P non-financial messages, routed directly to the payer requesting
they initiated a direct credit to the payee for the amount requested. There is
potential for fraud/scamming that needs to be addressed.

Savings

Kenyans in comparison to the Work Bank's categories of world and developed countries are significant savers at 67% (Table 9.8).

As expected, mobile money accounts are used by 37% of the population
followed by savings club or with individuals outside of the family. Financial
institution at 21% is the third choice. The world and developing countries
do not use mobile money accounts. Firstly, the percentage of actors saving in
those categories are approximately two-thirds the Kenya level. This could be
a reflection of income levels but also the trust factor.

Younger Kenyans are also likely to save over the other two categories
which would be expected to deliver a bias toward mobile money accounts.

Not Only M-Pesa

When it comes to Kenya payment services, the mind focuses immediately onto
M-Pesa but as Vincent Matinde explained in his article, 'Kenya's Digital Payment System is to Fragment', published on the https://itweb.africa/website,
there are other payment options available, although M-Pesa is dominant.

Vincent quotes Francis Mugane, General Manager at Interswitch Speak-
ing at the #WhatsNextMettaNBO forum hosted by Metta Nairob;

"This fragmentation clutters up the payment till. In terms of backend and
reconciliation, the investment the merchant must make is very high for (it)
to be sustained. Because they are working with several different partners

TABLE 9.8 Where Do Kenyans Save

	Kenya	Developing	World
Saved money	67%	42%	49%
Club or person outside family	32%	9%	–
Financial institution	21%	23%	29%
Mobile money	37%	4%	3%
Young age	67%	41%	45%
Older age	32%	43%	50%

Source: World Bank Group, World Bank Group – Global Findex Database

they don't even benefit from the economies of scale, because you are negotiating different prices with different partners."

Francis Mugane further stated that:

"The Kenyan consumer can make use of several options for digital payment including: mVisa, M-Pesa till numbers, M-Pesa 1Tap, Airtel Money, T-Kash from Telkom Kenya, Visa cards, M-Pesa Bank Transfer with various bank applications, payment through supermarkets point system and PesaLink."

Together these constitute 33% of the payments compared to over 60% generated through cash, according to statistics from Naivas Supermarkets.

Vincent goes onto to quote Willie Kimani, Chief Commercial Officer of Naivas Limited who confirmed that card payment constitutes about 17%, while M-Pesa payment is still at 16%. Cash is over 60%, while the balance is corporate purchases through bank transfers.

It must be recognized that these statements were made in March 2018. What is the current situation?

Mobile Money Services

A competitor to Safaricom (the mobile operator who launched M-Pesa) is Airtel who has launched a competitive mobile money service, Airtel Money. Airtel Africa issued a prospectus in June 2019 which provided a brief but detailed profile of the Kenya mobile market. Key points being:

- Mobile penetration 2018 equalled 92% with churn of 3%
- Connections in 2018 reaching 47.8 million
- MFS (Mobile Financial Services) 74% penetration of total connections
- Kenya's average user's activity was in 2018 stated as USD342 per month, up from USD327 per month in 2016.
- Mobile market has four providers, Safaricom with 63% market share and Airtel at 28%
- MFS market is expected to reach 53.6 million users in 2023 with an adoption level of 85% of connections

Airtel Mobile Money

Airtel Mobile Money is explained on the Airtel Kenya website. The services offered are:

- International funds transfers to Airtel subscribers in Rwanda, Tanzania, Zambia & Malawi

- Short-term unsecured loans for account holders that satisfy certain criteria who have been a subscriber for a specified period
- Mobile Money interoperability providing for registered subscribers the ability to transfer funds to Safaricom subscribers
- Transfer of funds between Airtel Money and a bank account
- Lipa Na Airtel is a service supporting both merchant purchases and bill payment
- Account balance enquiry is supported

M-Pesa

Safaricom's mobile money service is M-Pesa. The scope of the services is available on https://www.safaricom.co.ke/personal/m-pesa. The services covered are:

- Checking account balance
- Cash deposits at agents
- Cash withdrawals at both ATMs and agents
- Money transfer
- Lipa Na M-Pesa which supports bill payment and purchases at merchants
- Hikikisha is a service enabling senders to confirm the name of the intended recipient prior to completing a money transfer

India – Full Function NPS

The Indian model for Financial Inclusion is based on extending the NPS to reach the financially excluded. Referred to as PMJDY, the following initiatives have been implemented:

- Aadhaar, a card scheme that links each citizen to their name and address by assigning a 12-digit number
- PMJDY, basic savings account scheme
- RuPay, domestic payment card scheme supporting both debit and credit products
- Accident insurance
- Mudra Card, provides credit to the micro enterprise sector plus both personal accident and permanent disability insurance

The PMJDY scheme is based on financial institution accounts, supported by the standard NPS channels. A cornerstone to the scheme has been the introduction of banking correspondents (BC) who are aligned to a bank, operating their own network of agents. These agents reach out to those at the bottom of the socio-economic pyramid. They bridge the 'last mile'.

TABLE 9.9 Impact of BC Model

	2011	2014	2017	2021
Adults with an account	35%	53%	80%	78%

Source: World Bank Group, World Bank Group – Global Findex Database

The impact of the BC model can be seen in the growth of account holders as reported in the World Bank Group Findex Database (Table 9.9).

These numbers are impressive. India having 78% of its adult population having an account in 2021 means it has more than doubled in the last ten years, reported as 35% in the Findex database in 2011.

The Reserve Bank of India with the PMJDY scheme have pursued the financial institution account model and not the mobile money account model. For India, mobile accounts only appear in the World Bank Group Index in 2021 with a percentage of 10%. This may explain the 1% variance that appears in the World Bank Group Index in 2021 between accounts and financial institution accounts, but it can be concluded that the 9% of the adult banked population have both types of accounts.

The 2% decline in accounts between 2017 and 2021 can be attributed to several factors including Covid-19, where the number of new accounts opened by those individuals becoming adults dropped is a plausible reason.

Account Activity

Having a significant percentage of the population with a bank account as stated previously is fundamentally meaningless unless those accounts are being used. This is the challenge for all Financial Inclusion programs.

The information release, 1749749 from the Ministry of Finance states, "PMJDY Accounts have grown three-fold from 14.72 Crore in Mar'15 to 43.04 Crore as on 18-08-2021". The Ministry of Finance reports that 86% are operative. The Ministry also reports that RuPay cards have been issued to 31.23 Core PMJDY account holders.

The information release states that the PMJDY scheme has been launched on what is referred to as the 6 pillars:

- Universal access to banking services – Branch and BC
- Basic savings bank accounts with overdraft facility of Rs. 10,000/- to every eligible adult
- Financial Literacy Program – Promoting savings, use of ATMs, getting ready for credit, availing insurance, and pensions, using basic mobile phones for banking
- Creation of Credit Guarantee Fund – To provide banks some guarantee against defaults

- Insurance – Accident covers up to Rs. 1,00,000 and life cover of Rs. 30,000 on account opened between 15 August 2014 to 31 January 2015
- Pension scheme for Unorganized sector

Further the release states the objectives as being:

'Pradhan Mantri Jan-Dhan Yojana (PMJDY) is National Mission for Financial Inclusion to ensure access to financial services, namely, Banking/Savings & Deposit Accounts, Remittance, Credit, Insurance, Pension in an affordable manner.'

Objectives

Ensure access of financial products & services at an affordable cost
Use of technology to lower cost & widen reach

Basic tenets of the scheme

Banking the unbanked – Opening of basic savings bank deposit (BSBD) account with minimal paperwork, relaxed KYC, e-KYC, account opening in camp mode, zero balance, & zero charges.

Securing the unsecured – Issuance of indigenous debit cards for cash withdrawals & payments at merchant locations, with free accident insurance coverage of Rs. 2 lakhs

Funding the unfunded – Other financial products like micro-insurance, overdraft for consumption, micro-pension, & micro-credit

Aadhaar – Citizen Identification

This program was launched in 2008 with the focus on documenting every citizen and holding a record on a single database. Each Aadhaar card links a unique 12-digit identification number to the scanned images of the holders IRIS and fingerprints.

Time (India) – Billy Perrigo on September 28, 2018, reported:

On Wednesday, that began to change. India's Supreme Court, in a landmark ruling, said that private companies could no longer require users to provide their Aadhaar details as a condition of service.

The same court also upheld the legality of the system, saying it does not violate Indians' right to privacy and could therefore continue to operate. "Aadhaar gives dignity to the marginalized," the judges on the Court's bench said. "Dignity to the marginalized outweighs privacy."

It has also been made clear by the authorities that Aadhaar is not a citizen identification system. Therefore, Aadhaar simply links a person to their name and address. What is important is Aadhaar can authenticate the holder. Further, eAadhaar, a digitally signed electronic copy, has the validity of the physical card.

The Aadhaar Brochure July 2022 informs us that 93% saturation level has been reached or 133.0530 crore have been issued. Authentications undertaken is at 7358.44 crore; plus 77.25 crore bank accounts have been linked to Aadhaar on NPCI (National Payments Corporation of India) mapper plus 1,400 crore transactions AePs. These take on real meaning when it is realized that a crore equals 10 million.

The Aadhaar holds a citizen's name, gender, date of birth and address.

Aadhaar has allowed Indian citizens who may previously have not been able to open a bank account because of KYC to be in a position where they now can.

PMJDY Accounts

PMJDY is an initiative of the Indian government to provide financial services to those occupying the lower levels of the socio-economic pyramid, specifically to enable financial accounts to be opened.

RuPay

The third component of the Indian solution has been the issuance of a domestic payment card scheme supporting both debit and credit products. A scheme modelled in part on Visa and MasterCard with an expanded or broader vision.

RuPay illustrates that the development of the Indian payment system has been broad based covering all levels of the socio-economic pyramid. The card products on offer are a complete mix meeting the needs of the wealthy down to the lower levels of the pyramid such as farmers requiring a micro credit facility. The card products are issued by a broad base of banks (if not all banks) covering:

- Credit
- Debit
- Payroll
- Student
- Virtual

The NPCI supports the following services:

- National Financial Switch, supporting interoperability between financial institutions
- CTS, Cheque Truncation System

- Bharat Interface Money (BHIM). NPCI supports a Unified Payment Interface (UPI), which is a mobile services platform. Using a Payee's UPI ID, account number, Aadhaar, or a QR scan, funds can be sent using the BHIM mobile application. Request Money as well as Scan & Pay are also transaction types. Reference www.bhimupi.org.in for more details.
- Bharat Bill Payment System (BBPS). This is a system where registered billers can instruct their customers to pay electronically (digitally). Billers can be online to the service, provide a file of bills due. Bills can be paid through multiple channels:

  - Agents
  - Business Correspondents
  - Internet
  - Kiosk
  - ATM
  - Mobile

Bills can be paid using a range of card products and UPI (Unified Payment Interface) accessing funds held at the payer's financial institutions.

Mudra Card

The Mudra (Micro Units Development & Refinance Agency) debit card (Pradhan Mantri Mudra Yojana scheme) is an initiative of the Indian government to provide credit to the micro enterprise sector. Loans are distributed through partnering institutions. This scheme provides a working capital facility that the card/account holder can access to develop their business in an efficient and affordable manner. The card also provides both personal accident and permanent disability insurance cover of Rs.1 Lakh.

There is a switch away from the public banks and other institutions to the private banks (Table 9.10). Will this develop into a longer-term trend where the private sector will gain dominance of this financial inclusion lending sector?

TABLE 9.10 Loan Categories

Type	Description
Shishu	For start-up, first-time entrepreneurs – Up to Rs 50,000
Kishor	Entrepreneurs with existing business –From Rs 50,000 to 5 Lakh
Tarun	Businessman loans for expansion- From Rs 5 Lakh up to 10 Lakh Total Number and Value

Source: World Bank Group, World Bank Group – Global Findex Database

There are three categories of loans:

Reference the Mudra Annual Report 2020–2021, www.mudra.org.in for details.

The Mudra lending facility is designed to enable:

- Cultivation of crops
- Marketing expenses
- Farmer household costs
- Working capital to enable farm maintenance work, etc.
- Investment credit requirement for agriculture Opposing Approaches – Is there a Preference?

Jurisdiction View

The following data extracted from the World Bank Group Findex Database 2021 raises questions as well as answers a few.

If a citizen is paid in cash they can be expected to spend it as cash and may only then deposit any surplus into an account (Table 9.11).

If the premise that to encourage citizens to use digital payment services they must first have funds in their account is logically correct, then wages and government payments must be deposited into accounts is a prerequisite. The Table 9.11 below indicates that India has been achieving approximately 39% for wages, 55% for pensions of this objective. Those countries with more developed payment system are near to or over 90%.

TABLE 9.11 Received Digital Payment – Made Cash Payments

	2014	2017	2021
Made a deposit (% with a financial institution account, age 15+)	47%	42%	29%
Received wages: into an account (% of wage recipients, age 15+)	21%	32%	39%
Received government transfer or pension: into an account (% of government transfer or pension recipients, age 15+)		58%	55%
Received domestic remittances: into an account (% of recipients, age 15+)		31%	37%
Made a withdrawal (% with a financial institution account, age 15+)	40%	42%	39%
Made a utility payment: using cash only (% who paid utility bills, age 15+)	91%	62%	58%

Source: World Bank Group, World Bank Group – Global Findex Database

TABLE 9.12 Where Do Indians Save

	Population (age +15)	Account	Number of Accounts	Inactive Account	Number Has Inactive
2014	903,921,920	53%	479,078,618	17%	153,666,726
2017	954,547,392	80%	763,637,914	31%	295,909,692
2021	1,018,986,816	78%	794,809,716	27%	275,126,440

Source: World Bank Group, World Bank Group – Global Findex Database

Another key indicator is the percentage of those that used cash to pay utility bills. For India, since 2014 the percentage has dropped significantly from 91% to 58%. Many of the developed payment system countries are 5% or below with a select few at 0%.

Background to this is the growth in the adult population, which drives those that have an account and whose who have an inactive account. As the number of citizens who have an account grows, the percentage with inactive accounts has also grown over the seven-year period, 2014–2021. The percentage are also sourced from the World Bank Group Findex Database (Table 9.12).

The percentage of accounts declined in 2021 although 2% is statistically can be considered within the margin for error. Fundamentally it could be argued that the level of inclusion and the activity levels stayed static during a period that was impacted due to Covid-19.

The 2021 figures show the drop in cash being used. This again could have been impacted by Covid-19. The question is will cash over the next reporting period usage revert or will digital payments become entrenched?

Payment System Score Card, India vs Kenya

It is important to understand the different pathways these jurisdictions have taken, while recognizing they are two diverse countries with different needs, based especially on their respective size. India has a population of 1.353 billion and Kenya in comparison has a mere 51.4 million. In term of land mass, India is 3,287,263 square kilometres with a population density of 421 km square kilometre. Compared to Kenya 580,567 square kilometres, with a population density of 82 per square kilometre.

On these figures a comparison may seem inappropriate. Even more so when comparing GDP with India at USD2.719 trillion and Kenya at USD1.4 billion. These figures though become comparable when reviewing GDP per capita (World Bank, 2018) India is at USD 2,010.00, and the Kenya figure is USD 1,710.50. This reflects the rural population; India being 66% rural, with agriculture generating 16.2% of the GDP and in comparison, Kenya is 73% rural with agriculture contributing 30.2% of the GDP.

Based on the premise that addressing rural Financial Inclusion is more challenging because the infrastructure in terms of basic services is poor, both countries are in a similar position. Kenya is more dependent on agriculture (higher GDP contribution) than India so there must be more economic justification for Kenya to invest in the development of rural communities.

Based on the World Bank Global Findex Database 2021 data, Appendix A; Transition to Digital Kenya scored 4.11 with a global position of 45th out of 124 countries who participated in the survey. India in comparison was scored at 1.73 with a global position of 78th. This is an indication of where each country is position in respective to their development programs.

The following data is extracted from the World Bank Global Findex Database 2021. This World Bank data is for the category, 'Lower Middle Income' (Table 9.13).

TABLE 9.13 India/Kenya Payment Score Cardle

Score Card Classifications	India	Kenya
Account (% age 15+)	78%	79%
Account, rural (% age 15+)	77%	75%
Financial institution account (% age 15+)	77%	51%
Debit card ownership (% age 15+)	27%	22%
Mobile money account (% age 15+)	10%	69%
Received wages in the past year (% age 15+)	20%	36%
Received wages in the past year, rural (% age 15+)	19%	35%
Received wages: into a financial institution account (% age 15+)	6%	17%
Received wages: through a mobile phone (% wage recipient, age 15+)	2%	33%
Received wages: in cash only (% wage recipients, age 15+)	59%	30%
Received government transfers in the past year (% age 15+)	8%	12%
Received government transfers in the past year, rural (% age 15+)	9%	12%
Received payments for agricultural products in the past year (% age 15+)	14%	34%
Received payments for agricultural products in the past year, rural (% age 15+)	17%	37%
Received payments for agricultural products: into a financial institution account (% payment recipient, age 15+)	19%	18%
Received payments for agricultural products: into a financial institution account (% payment recipient, age 15+)	22%	46%
Received payments for agricultural products: through a mobile phone (% payment recipient, age 15+)	2%	37%
Received payments for agricultural products: in cash only (% payment recipients, age 15+)	60%	51%
Borrowed from a financial institution (% age 15+)	7%	17%

(*Continued*)

TABLE 9.13 (Continued)

Score Card Classifications	India	Kenya
Sent or received domestic remittances in the past year (% age 15+)	19%	67%
Sent or received domestic remittances in the past year, rural (% age 15+)	20%	66%
Sent or received domestic remittances: using an account (% age 15+)	7%	59%
Sent or received domestic remittances: through a mobile phone (% age 15+)	1%	63%
Sent or received domestic remittances: in person and in cash only (% age 15+)	8%	1%
Received domestic remittances: through a financial institution (% age 15+)	5%	15%
Received domestic remittances: using an account (% recipients, age 15+)	31%	90%
Received domestic remittances: through a financial institution (% recipients, age 15+)	31%	28%
Received domestic remittances: in person and in cash only (% recipients, age 15+)	51%	1%
Received domestic remittances: through a money transfer service (% recipients, age 15+)	2%	1%
Received domestic remittances: through an over-the-counter service (% recipients, age 15+)	3%	7%
Received domestic remittances: through a mobile phone (% recipients, age 15+)	2%	94%
Used a mobile phone or the internet to access a financial institution account in the past year (% with a financial institution account, age 15+)	6%	57%
Deposit in the past year (% with a financial institution account, age 15+)	42%	73%

Source: World Bank Group, World Bank Group – Global Findex Database

Key Findings

Both countries have high levels of account penetration, the first step in Financial Inclusion.

The high level of citizen identification cards removes the KYC impediment to opening an account.

The statistics clearly identify where each country fits within the mobile/account divide. It is interesting that Kenya is dominated by mobile but there is still over 50% of the actors who have a financial institution account. Alternatively, India is clearly positioned as a bank dominant payment system country with 77% having financial accounts.

Kenyans are more likely to borrow funds and receive domestic remittances through digital channels than Indians. World Bank Index Database

2021: Sent or received domestic remittances: in person and in cash only, Kenyans 1%, Indians 8%.

As with remittances, the other categories for receiving payments are dominated by the mobile channel for Kenya. The exception is agricultural payments where for Kenya cash payments are at 51% and India is higher at 60%.

Bank or Mobile Module

The answer is not black and white, as it depends on whether a country is playing a short- or a long-term game. Can mobile provide quicker short-term benefits than the bank model? Will account holders switch from using mobile money accounts to using financial institution accounts once they are comfortable with digital services because of the broader service offering. Banks in all jurisdiction struggle (assuming they even attempt) to deliver service to remote (rural) districts.

India has gone to a holistic approach in terms of developing NPS and therefore offering a full range of financial services. The banking correspondent model address the remote district challenge. Kenya's approach could be argued to be more organic (less planned) as the mobile money transfer service has driven the financial inclusion program. Only those that initiated M-Pesa, can answer the question of whether they had a long-term view the program would drive financial inclusion. Was it simply a case of using the technology to address an immediate problem concerning the cost and reliability of the existing domestic remittance delivery services?

Without doubt M-Pesa was adopted by Kenyans and quickly used for money transfer, p2p, p2b, etc. M-Pesa has also been used for savings as the funds were not always fully withdrawn. The Kenya FinAccess Household Survey Report demonstrates that not one service caters for all needs. Since M-Pesa was introduced, the impact on the percentage of the population adopting banking services has more than doubled. Banks have also received a boost through the introduction of mobile banking.

The point being whether the goal is more likely to be achieved by delivering Financial Inclusion through the development of a NPS that allows all citizens to transact with each other, regardless of where they reside on the socio-economic pyramid. The India model is more planned than the Kenyan model, based on a strategy to deliver financial inclusion and improved financial services for all citizens.

Bibliography

Aadhaar Brochure, July 2022. www.scribd.com/document/672383320/Aadhaar-Brochure-Sep-23-1

Boaten, Kwadwo, Financial Inclusion for Economic Growth – An Overview of Some Financial Inclusion Policies in India. *KAAV International, Journal of Economics, Commerce & Business Management*, March 2018.

Digital Payments Adoption in India, NPCI Digital Payments Adoption 2020.

FinAccess Houshold Survey report 2021 (date modified 1/6/2022).

Focus Economics, Indicators, 2019.

GSMA, State of the Industry Report on Mobile Money, 2018/2019/2020/2021.

Matinde, Vicent, Kenya's Digital Payment System is to Fragmented, 29 March 2018.

Mudra Annual Report, 2020/2021.

Perrigo, Billy, What to Know About Aadhaar, India's Biometric Identity System. *Time*, September 2018.

PMJDY Statistics, 2021–2022.

Reserve Bank of India, *Annual Report, 2021–2022*.

Telpo, What Is a Micro A, 6 July 2021.World Bank Group, Global Findex Database, 2021/17/14/11.

10

DIGITAL CASH – USER PROPOSITION

There are various forms of digital currency being promoted to the payment sector. CBDC, which stands for central bank digital currency is in various stages of exploration by various country central banks. Other promoters are using terms such as crypto, stable currency, and digital coins.

CBDC is fundamentally outside the scope of this book, but it is important to recognize the interest. Several, if not all central banks have recognized that with the decline in cash usage the effectiveness of monetary policy has been weakened. Money deposited in financial institution accounts is viewed by the payment sector as private money and often labelled electronic money.

Digital cash can be considered as electronic money but resides in an account outside the traditional financial system. Its real value proposition is unclear with NRT supported by R2P being introduced into mainstream payment platforms.

What prudential supervision is being provided to holders of digital cash? This is a critical question if DC deposit holders are to be protected.

Digital Cash Proposition

The digital cash proposition for the retail economy is difficult to determine unless being promoted as a secured method of transferring funds through what is an end-to-end open network. Promoters of digital cash in many cases are promoting their solutions to smaller economies (countries) where the financially excluded or the number of citizens at the lower levels of the socio-economic pyramid is proportionally high.

DOI: 10.4324/9781003471073-10

The following are points of interest:

- Digital cash providers are promoting their accounts/wallets as an alternative to financial institutions accounts. Digital cash value is often begged to the official currency of the domicile country. The challenge is how to deposit and access funds if the digital cash service is not integrated into the NPS?
- The need for actors to have a smartphone. If this is the case, a high percentage of the financially excluded will continue to be excluded.
- An advantage being promoted by one or more providers is no fees as there is no entity in the middle of a transfer, clipping the ticket. If blockchain technology is being used with multiple distributed ledgers, there needs to be a robust business case. Costs must be recovered and this needs to be explained.
- Blockchain and distributed ledgers plus other features should address any fraud issue(s). This may be the case if the system is closed but there must a channel to transfer funds into/out of digital cash other than an agency network.
- Digital cash is attempting to be like cash supporting anonymity. Payment transfers cannot be traced. This factor goes against KYC and AML principles. With high levels of scamming and fraud to achieve a positive point of difference, digital cash must have a strong point of difference.

Wallet Holder Proposition

In discussing any new payment method, the key success factor at the top of the list is always a strong actor proposition. Does digital cash have a strong actor proposition in the retail sector? Retailers are increasingly looking for a frictionless payment method where funds become available immediately. An issue was raised in a Pacific Island country where a digital cash pilot had been deployed is merchant acceptance. Digital cash holders were looking to convert their funds into physical cash, but merchants experienced delays in settlement from the scheme operators. Merchants not holding sufficient cash is a common issue across all forms of digital/electronic payments where merchants are acting as a 'cash out' agent.

Could digital cash acceptance be improved if supported by an NRT platform and potentially be converted to private/electronic money (or alternatively private money converted to digital cash) for depositing in the payee's financial repository held at an institution under prudential supervision? Then why introduce digital cash and not stay with electronic money? The point of difference between these two forms of money becomes unclear.

This introduces a multi-currency economy where funds transition between the payer/payee based on the commercial needs of the participating parties. A use case for digital cash potentially is in supporting business critical transactions, protecting a payment from being disputed in a legal context is a strong proposition. If distributed ledgers are being used, the tracing of a money transfer is feasible, supported by a strong crypto regime.

The application of digital cash in a financial system context is not clear. There is physical cash, electronic or private money, and CBDC potentially for high value payments, so is there a need for another exchange of value method.

Introducing Digital Authentication

Real cash does not need or at least does not support the authentication of the holder as the actual owner of the funds, only they are in possession. Digital cash should require account holder authentication, preferably biometric (means of unique physical characteristics) such as facial recognition, fingerprints, and voice recognition.

Distributing Aid or Disaster Relieve Money

Digital cash is being proposed as a method of distributing aid money in the case of a natural disaster, to the vulnerable citizens in need. This use case has the potential to ensure funds are being transferred to the intended individual/ family. The recipients would likely need to have a digital cash wallet installed on their mobile handset or if not need to install a wallet app to enable the acceptance. The security elements of the transfer must ensure the digital cash is deposited in the intended wallet.

As mentioned above, the recipient will look to covert digital cash to cash through an agency network. Alternately when making a purchase they will look for a cash out option. In effect it is the same scenario that has been experienced by mobile money providers were cash out dominates post the receipt of a remittance crediting a mobile money account. There needs to be an extensive effort to build up an agency network but more importantly a merchant base that will accept digital cash as a form of payment, removing the need for cash.

This is what an NRT platform supporting a network of acceptance devices, potentially what a mobile handset can deliver.

An alternative is building up a cash dispenser network (ATMs) but this introduces a challenge regarding servicing the devices, particularly cash replenishment. This network may have a short-term need if the adoption of digital cash by local communities was rapid. Past experiences would suggest that this will not be the case.

Is digital cash a technology solution looking for a problem? It appears that the unbanked or underserved are the targets for many promoting digital cash, more so than CBDC. It is difficult to accept that crypto/digital cash is going to address the financial inclusion challenges. For those who have been in the payments business several years, it is not surprising that 'here we go again' is thought, if not spoken.

A further factor is that digital currency is a very immature payment method. Before and if it becomes mainstream it will go through further iterations of development, which will raise a challenge for smaller economies who are unable to justify future system upgrades. Cost of ownership of a payment system can be considerable and is only justifiable if supported by high transaction volume.

Technologist and their followers need to consider the digital cash proposition over electronic money. Digital cash is promoted as having the same value as electronic money which is the same as cash. Digital cash is to be stored in a wallet, like a financial account. The wallet may be held on a mobile handset but if so must be backed up on a central database in case of a handset failure and the need to be restored.

Digital cash cannot be expected to shift actors in the low-income category because of the requirement to have access to technology but may assist those in the low to medium income categories to move up within the socio-economic pyramid.

11

OBSERVATIONS AND FINAL COMMENT

Building a national financial system (inclusive of payments) that services all the actors in an economy is an extremely challenging exercise. There is no question that an NPS that reaches out to all actors will benefit a country's economy and improve the wellness of all.

What appears to be a serious issue is that those responsible for the NPS are not developing a strategy supported by an architectural plan to achieve both short and long-term objectives (goals). A road map to support the implementation of the strategy is required. There are many almost random short-term objectives often driven by the most recent FinTech organization to arrive in a developing country, often support by an NGO prepared to fund a project.

These may be strong if not extreme words, but we need to go back to the transportation parallels discussed in, <u>National Payment & Transportation Systems Face Similar Challenges</u>.

Nobody would purchase a motor vehicle designed to be used on a network of roads if the roads did not exist or the roads that have been built started nowhere and finished nowhere, with nowhere in between. So why would anybody open an account when there is no efficient means of deposited funds and there is very limited opportunity for acceptance or for value to be transferred? The actor proposition must be strong.

Strategy

The strategy for an NPS must be built on a framework that facilitates pathways between the various communities that make up the socio-economic pyramid. Starting small and rolling out, interconnected services based on a

DOI: 10.4324/9781003471073-11

hub and spoke model with the Central Bank being at the centre with their ESAS accounts. The payment platform, supporting subsidiary payment services that may overtime be extended, merged, or dropped as new payment services are added, consolidated, or simply phased out. Satellite payment services that are unconnected (or cannot be connected because of their technical design) to the NPS must not be allowed to be established. If they already exist, enforce them to comply to regulations within a realistic period.

There are and will need to be payment services that meet the needs of specific sectors of the population, consumers, or businesses but they must have a 'back door' to the NPS. Generally, these services will have been designed to meet the unique or specific needs at the point of acceptance and potentially to collect and transmit specific data supporting the payment instructions.

History of Going Nowhere

Historically the payment sector has seen:

1 Smart card closed loop systems that have disappeared into history. A few may still exist but even the most successful in the transit sector are being replaced by NFC-enabled card scheme plastic/chips or mobile. They have been open to accepting payment (scheme) cards.
2 Next came proprietary closed loop mobile money services. Services developed by MNOs exclusively for their subscriber base. These services with one or two exceptions have not meet expectations.
3 Now the payments market is seeing the emergence of closed loop digital cash systems.
4 What will be next? Smart cards, mobile money, and digital cash all have a common aspect. Their existence has been driven by a belief that their success (even if the proposition is unclearly defined) will be driven by the acceptance of the technology.

These services would have more success if they were designed to be open and not closed. The ability to migrate these services to being open will obviously vary dependent on their design. However, to transition will require additional investment and based on the experience of the author, many MNOs specifically have not been prepared to entertain additional funding for underperforming mobile money services.

Infrastructure

Infrastructure presents a challenge for many at the lower levels of the socio-economic pyramid. The ability to service remote locations with no mobile coverage but where the electricity grid also does not reach. There must be acceptance that inhabitants of very remote locations will always be disadvantaged with respect to Financial Inclusion. But this could be their life style choice.

The electricity grid in many countries is government-owned or heavily regulated, and as suggested in this book, such governments should also own the mobile network or stipulate a condition to holding an MNO licence is to provide full coverage that supports digital messaging. Owning a mobile handset is no longer an option but has become a device that greatly contributes to an individual's participation in society and their quality of life. Governments in many countries do set up enterprises to manage infrastructure services, operating commercially but with a social mandate.

Social Connection

Social connection is also a key element of developing Financial Inclusion. Financial services have been developed in many countries to meet the needs and behavioural patterns of the middle and upper-income classes. Educated and earning an income, ensuring a quality of life, supported by money transfer (financial) services.

In this book, there is referral to banking correspondents who support agents in communities that are open when the residents are home. They live in the community and know the customers. It is the same case for the informal financial institutions where they service the needs of their communities.

Financial services must reach out to the lower income communities, they cannot expect these communities to reach out to them. This is not only physically but also socially.

Final Comment

With new payment services the question must be asked, what is the account holder proposition. Recognizing that the competition is most often cash. Why should citizens switch to a digital form of cash? Being a clever technology-based solution is not a reason. Blockchain or CBDC is not understood by most people.

For financial inclusion programs to be successful they must have a very strong and compelling actor proposition. In this book the success factors and needs of the citizens is covered. Possibly a greater understanding is required of how communities internally interact and how they connect to other communities is required. This is strictly not a payment issue but a social issue. Payments is just one of the social/community threads.

APPENDIX 1

Country League Table

The following map and supporting table are based on selective higher-level responses from the World Bank Global Findex Database, 2021. Responses covering the percentage of adults who have an account. For example, a lower level of accounts produces a lower score.

Jurisdiction	Score	Ranking
Estonia	7.45	1
Latvia	6.62	2
Denmark	6.59	3
Norway	6.57	4
Czech Republic	6.54	5
Sweden	6.35	6
Singapore	6.30	7
Slovak Republic	6.26	8
Mongolia	6.26	9
Iceland	6.23	10
Finland	6.14	11
Netherlands	6.08	12
New Zealand	5.99	13
China	5.96	14
Poland	5.96	15
Canada	5.93	16
Belgium	5.82	17
Korea, Rep.	5.81	18
Thailand	5.77	19
Greece	5.77	20
Australia	5.77	21

(Continued)

(Continued)

Jurisdiction	Score	Ranking
Ireland	5.70	22
United Kingdom	5.60	23
Austria	5.57	24
Germany	5.47	25
Russian Federation	5.45	26
Lithuania	5.41	27
Spain	5.40	28
Switzerland	5.27	29
France	5.12	30
Hong Kong SAR, China	5.04	31
Slovenia	5.04	32
Hungary	5.01	33
United States	4.92	34
Israel	4.81	35
Italy	4.79	36
Malta	4.71	37
Chile	4.71	38
Croatia	4.60	39
Venezuela, RB	4.48	40
Portugal	4.43	41
Japan	4.40	42
Ukraine	4.19	43
Cyprus	4.13	44
Kenya	4.11	45
Malaysia	4.09	46
Brazil	4.05	47
South Africa	3.99	48
Kazakhstan	3.94	49
Iran, Islamic Rep.	3.89	50
Bulgaria	3.76	51
Mauritius	3.75	52
Saudi Arabia	3.62	53
Serbia	3.51	54
North Macedonia	3.45	55
Türkiye	3.31	56
United Arab Emirates	3.10	57
Uruguay	3.10	58
Argentina	2.96	59
Gabon	2.91	60
Ghana	2.87	61
Namibia	2.86	62
Uganda	2.70	63
Costa Rica	2.67	64
Romania	2.66	65
Bosnia and Herzegovina	2.63	66

(*Continued*)

(Continued)

Jurisdiction	Score	Ranking
Sri Lanka	2.43	67
Zimbabwe	2.26	68
Georgia	2.20	69
Jamaica	2.10	70
Bolivia	2.09	71
Senegal	2.09	72
Moldova	2.07	73
Ecuador	1.82	74
Tanzania	1.81	75
Colombia	1.78	76
Cameroon	1.73	77
India	1.73	78
Cote d'Ivoire	1.67	79
Philippines	1.67	80
Peru	1.65	81
Mozambique	1.59	82
Armenia	1.59	83
Liberia	1.58	84
Kosovo	1.57	85
Zambia	1.56	86
Paraguay	1.48	87
Benin	1.48	88
Togo	1.48	89
Myanmar	1.45	90
Bangladesh	1.41	91
Congo, Rep.	1.37	92
Mali	1.25	93
Indonesia	1.24	94
Malawi	1.24	95
Uzbekistan	1.19	96
Panama	1.15	97
Dominican Republic	1.14	98
Nigeria	1.11	99
Nepal	1.10	100
Kyrgyz Republic	0.99	101
Burkina Faso	0.96	102
Jordan	0.95	103
Morocco	0.92	104
Honduras	0.90	105
Albania	0.87	106
Lao PDR	0.75	107
Guinea	0.72	108
El Salvador	0.71	109
Algeria	0.71	110
Tajikistan	0.70	111

(Continued)

(Continued)

Jurisdiction	Score	Ranking
Tunisia	0.67	112
Sierra Leone	0.65	113
Cambodia	0.62	114
West Bank and Gaza	0.55	115
Nicaragua	0.47	116
Egypt, Arab Rep.	0.37	117
Pakistan	0.34	118
Iraq	0.32	119
Sierra Leone	0.32	120
Lebanon	0.27	121
Niger	0.25	122
Afghanistan	0.11	123
South Sudan	0.07	124

APPENDIX 2

Cash Dependency Indicators

The following table, like Appendix A, is based on the World Bank Global Findex Database, 2021, considering the percentage of adults who have an account. The higher the score, the greater dependency on cash payments.

It should be recognized that these indicators are a result of two factors:

- A country must have developed a National Payment System (NPS) that enables their citizens to reduce their dependency on cash.
- The citizen of a country must have adapted to using the digital payment services available.

For example, New Zealand on this table is ranked 2nd but in the previous league table it is 13th. This implies their NPS is not as developed as other countries, but the services available are used extensively. Canada is in a similar situation, ranked at 8th here but ranked at 18th in the league table.

The two top countries in the league table are Estonia and Latvia and are ranked in the cash dependency table at 18 and 48 respectively. However, Denmark and Norway at 3 and 4 in the league table have low cash dependency in this table with rankings of 6 and 1 respectively. Why is this the case? The only possible explanation is the maturity level of the digital services, and the level of adoption may be broad based, but the services may not be universally available across the respective economies.

Jurisdiction	Score	Ranking
Norway	0.00	1
New Zealand	0.01	2
Belgium	0.01	3
Austria	0.01	4
Finland	0.01	5
Denmark	0.01	6
Iceland	0.02	7
Canada	0.02	8
Netherlands	0.02	9
Sweden	0.02	10
France	0.04	11
Australia	0.05	12
United Kingdom	0.05	13
Germany	0.05	14
Afghanistan	0.06	15
Estonia	0.07	16
Niger	0.07	17
United States	0.08	18
Slovenia	0.09	19
Ireland	0.10	20
Spain	0.11	21
Switzerland	0.12	22
China	0.12	23
Lebanon	0.12	24
Sierra Leone	0.13	25
Italy	0.13	26
Korea, Rep.	0.13	27
Japan	0.15	28
Pakistan	0.15	29
Iran, Islamic Rep.	0.15	30
Congo, Rep.	0.17	31
Portugal	0.17	32
Burkina Faso	0.17	33
West Bank and Gaza	0.17	34
Mozambique	0.17	35
Honduras	0.17	36
Guinea	0.18	37
Iraq	0.18	38
Nicaragua	0.19	39
Malta	0.19	40
Mali	0.19	41
Hong Kong SAR, China	0.19	42
Venezuela, RB	0.20	43
Mongolia	0.20	44
Sierra Leone	0.20	45

(*Continued*)

(Continued)

Jurisdiction	Score	Ranking
Malawi	0.20	46
Saudi Arabia	0.21	47
Latvia	0.21	48
Bangladesh	0.24	49
Cote d'Ivoire	0.24	50
United Arab Emirates	0.24	51
Tanzania	0.25	52
Benin	0.25	53
Singapore	0.25	54
Liberia	0.26	55
Cyprus	0.26	56
Zimbabwe	0.26	57
Panama	0.27	58
Egypt, Arab Rep.	0.27	59
El Salvador	0.28	60
India	0.29	61
Israel	0.29	62
Zambia	0.29	63
Tunisia	0.30	64
Algeria	0.30	65
Jordan	0.31	66
Senegal	0.32	67
Gabon	0.32	68
Namibia	0.33	69
Dominican Republic	0.33	70
Costa Rica	0.33	71
Kenya	0.33	72
Cameroon	0.34	73
Poland	0.35	74
Morocco	0.35	75
Nigeria	0.35	76
Tajikistan	0.36	77
Slovak Republic	0.38	78
Colombia	0.40	79
Togo	0.40	80
Malaysia	0.40	81
Uganda	0.40	82
Czech Republic	0.41	83
Türkiye	0.41	84
Lithuania	0.42	85
Peru	0.42	86
Paraguay	0.43	87
Greece	0.44	88
Uzbekistan	0.44	89
Kazakhstan	0.44	90

(*Continued*)

(Continued)

Jurisdiction	Score	Ranking
North Macedonia	0.45	91
Nepal	0.45	92
Georgia	0.46	93
Ecuador	0.46	94
Russian Federation	0.48	95
Brazil	0.49	96
Argentina	0.50	97
Lao PDR	0.50	98
South Africa	0.50	99
Chile	0.53	100
Armenia	0.53	101
Croatia	0.53	102
Uruguay	0.55	103
Jamaica	0.55	104
Cambodia	0.57	105
Kyrgyz Republic	0.58	106
Myanmar	0.62	107
Kosovo	0.62	108
Mauritius	0.62	109
Albania	0.64	110
Ghana	0.66	111
Hungary	0.67	112
Bolivia	0.70	113
Sri Lanka	0.71	114
Indonesia	0.72	115
Romania	0.75	116
Philippines	0.75	117
Ukraine	0.77	118
Thailand	0.78	119
Moldova	0.78	120
Bulgaria	0.86	121
Serbia	0.96	122
Bosnia and Herzegovina	0.96	123

APPENDIX 3

Definitions

Settlement Institutions (Direct Participant): An institution that holds a settlement account (ESAS) with the central bank for clearing and settlement purposes. The Settlement Institutions are primarily banks although increasingly larger non-settlement institutions, commercial organizations, and government institutions are being given the opportunity to become a settlement institution.

Normally organizations that represent a systemic risk to the payment system if they failed.

Non-Settlement Institutions (Indirect Participant): do not directly participate in the clearing and settlement process and therefore, are required to have a relationship with a settlement institution. These institutions are normally not full service. As an example, they may have a specific client base and be referred to as community bank, co-operative bank, building society, credit union, savings, and lending association, etc. PSPs also fall into this space.

Although not a settlement institution, they still fall under the central banks' governance regime.

Banking Correspondent: as defined in the financial inclusion sector, specifically used in India as a service provider delivering services on behalf of a bank. In the Indian environment, they offer no-frills banking services to the traditionally under or unbanked. They normally support an agency network and utilize mobile technology.

Mobile Operators: The mobile operators with respect to the legacy mobile money systems own the 'real estates' as these services are built for the basic and/or feature phones. The smartphones except for Apple, the handset 'real estate' is open to all. This is not the case with basic/feature phones as the MNOs control what applications reside on the SIM card.

Agency Network: Like a branch network, they are typically independently owned. Generally, for competitive reasons an agent will be aligned to one financial institution (or banking correspondent) and they do not support the concept of interoperability.

Near Real Time Payment (NRT) Systems: These are systems where the payer's account is debited immediately on receipt of their instruction by their financial institution. The corresponding credit request for an account hosted by another participating financial institution is then sent immediately to the NRT systems for the crediting of the payee's account. The crediting would be expected to occur on receipt of the transaction message. In an ideal world, this should occur within 60 seconds of the payer's bank receiving the instruction.

Faster Settlement System: NRT systems are now commonly supported by 'settlement before interchange'. In other words, on receipt of a request to credit a customer's account the payee's bank has already received the funds into their settlement account at the central bank. This process eliminates the systemic risk of the settlement process failing.

QR Codes: Stands for a Quick Response Code and is a 2D barcode. QR Codes supports the transfer of data between the originator and the recipient. Codes can be static and dynamic. The originator is required to display their code and the recipient must have the capability to scan and read the code.

QR Codes are being used for payments, specifically at the point of sale but not exclusively. The payer generally must have a Smartphone with an application that supports the reading and verification of a request to pay. However, there are various scheme with varying message flows.

The question of friction (time taken to complete a payment) especially when compared to other forms of initiating payment such as NFC.

Money Transfer: Payment transaction that involves one account being debit and a recipient account at the same or another financial institution being credited.

Not-On-Us: Receipt of a payment instruction where the contra transaction is to account with another financial institution.

Interchange: Process used when recipient account is at another institution, The process that supports not-on-us payment instructions.

Remittances: A money transfer transaction specifically referring to actors (often foreign workers) transferring funds to their family. Often cross borders but can also be domestic workers who have moved away from home to gain employment. Often in the cities.

Velocity of Money: The speed by which funds transition through the economy. If a product is sold in a market by a third party how soon will the funds be credited to the produces account, or the cash be received.

Digital Money: A form of electronic but often supported by cryptography that provides a layer of security. Often tokens and coins that can be aligned to ownership.

Digital Payments: A form of electronic payment through a network specifically supporting the electronic transfer of funds.

Interoperability: The term used when a payment service can connect to other payment services to support the transfer of funds between aligned payment services and financial institutions.

National Payment System (NPS): The payment system of a jurisdiction. Implies that there is interoperability between the services in a jurisdiction, at a level that supports the ability of an actor to transfer funds or receive funds from any other actor in the jurisdiction.

Digital Wallet: A repository for holding digital money that may exist on a device such as a mobile phone or microcircuit card or in the cloud. Based on the concept of a physical wallet.

Mobile Money Account: Is an account supported by a mobile service, normally a mobile operator. Traditionally been a closed loop service.

Financial Institution: General term for banks and other institution who have an exchange settlement account with the central bank. However not all banks have such an account and are considered indirect participants in the payment system.

Closed Network: Refers to telecommunication operator who does not support calls or data transfer to other operators in their jurisdiction.

Broadband: Broadband is a high-data-rate connection to the Internet. The technology gets its name because of the wide band of frequencies that is available for information transmission. Information can be multiplexed and sent on numerous channels, allowing more information to be transmitted at a given time. Dictionary - Techopedia

Narrowband: Narrowband refers to data communication and telecommunications tools, technologies, and services that utilize a narrower set or band of frequencies in the communication channel. These utilize the channel frequency that is considered flat or which will use a lesser number of frequency sets. Dictionary - Techopedia

Smartphones: Best described as a handheld computer, that can be connected to the Internet and support specifically designed software applications.

APPENDIX 4

Abbreviations

Abbreviation	Representation
AePs	Aadhar Enabled Payment System
AML	Anti-Money Laundering
API	Application Interface
ARPU	Average Revenue Per User
ATM	Automatic Teller Machine
BC	Banking Correspondent
BHIM	Bharat Interface Money
CBDC	Central Bank Digital Currency
CGAP	Consultative Group to Assist the Poor
CICO	Cash In Cash Out
CSD	Central System Depository
CTS	Cheque Truncation System
EFTPOS	Electronic Funds at Point of Sale
ESAS	Exchange Settlement Account
FP	Fast Payments
FSS	Fast Settlement System
G20	Group of Twenty (Governments)
GDP	Gross Domestic Product
GPFI	Global Partnership for Financial Inclusion
GSMA	Global System for Mobile Association
IBAN	International Bank Account Number
IP	Internet Protocol
ITU	International Telecommunication Union
KYC	Know Your Customer
IoT	Internet of Things
MFS	Mobile Financial Services
MNO	Mobile Network Operator

(Continued)

(Continued)

Abbreviation	Representation
MMOs	Mobile Money Operators
Mudra	Micro Units Development & Refinance Agency
NFC	Near Field Communications
NGO	Non-Government Organization
NPP	New Payment Platform (Australia)
NPS	National Payment System
NRT	Near Real Time
P2B	Person to Business
P2P	Person to Person
PBM	Personal Banking Machine
PMJDY	Pradhan Mantri Jan Dhan Yojana (Indian Financial Inclusion Program)
POS	Point of Sale
PSP	Payment Service Provider
RBI	Reserve Bank of India
ROI	Return on Investment
RTGS	Real Time Gross Settlement
SACCO	Savings and Credit Cooperative Organization
SIM	Subscriber Identity Module
UK	United Kingdom
UN	United Nations
UPI	Unified Payment Interface
USSD	Unstructured Supplementary Service Data

INDEX

Printed in the United States
by Baker & Taylor Publisher Services